Dialogue of Life

Bob McCahill

Dialogue of Life

A Christian among Allah's Poor

ORBIS BOOKS

Maryknoll, New York 10545

Copyright ©, text and photographs, 1996 by Bob McCahill, M.M.

Published by Orbis Books, Maryknoll, NY 10545-0308

Manufactured in the United States of America

ORBIS/ISBN 1-57075-066-1

For
Mom and Dad
Helen Rhodes-Cline and Harold Hector McCahill
my first teachers and God's best gift

Contents

Golenor, mother of a large extended family, rips apart a large, rough jackfruit with her bare hands for distribution among many expectant recipients. For a poor family this is a rare treat.

Preface

Between the ages of six and nineteen my ambition in life changed over a dozen times—from cartoonist to pilot, actor, archeologist, and so on—until the day I telephoned home from college to declare that I intended to become a missioner-priest. Dad answered that call. After hearing me out, he responded as he had to every other wholesome inclination I had ever voiced: "That's fine, son. We're all for it."

There was no question that God was calling me to *missionary* priesthood. In a moment of ecstasy which I experienced on October 31, 1956, in Seattle, Washington, and which continued to thrill my heart until the day I entered the seminary seven and a half months later, I became so conscious of divine love and magnanimity that I longed to give myself entirely to God—even to be promptly dissolved into God if that were possible. Only by becoming a missioner, I felt, could I hope to fulfill that yearning.

In 1964, after seven uneventful but happy years in the seminary, I was duly ordained and received my first assignment to the Philippines. There, on Mindanao, I found many opportunities for energetic service among the good, struggling people of the barrios and other remote areas. But after eleven exhilarating years among the poor of Mindanao, I received word from Maryknoll of the need for volunteers to begin working in Bangladesh.

About Bangladesh I knew little other than that it was near India and that it was constantly in the world news as the site of frequent natural disasters. But the call came at the right moment in my life. It made good sense to me that a missioner would leave one mission—in this case, the Philippines—in order to assist in another, needier mission. And so, in 1975, I left the Philippines behind to enter a new and unfamiliar world.

Until 1947 the place now known as Bangladesh had been part of India, and then, until 1971, part of Pakistan. In 1971 Bangladesh won its independence. At present in Bangladesh there are more than 120 million people, of whom approximately 86 percent are Muslims and 12 percent are Hindus. It is a crowded place. The area is equivalent to the state of Iowa, but with approximately forty times the population. Bangladesh is a rich deltic plain. Lush vegetation shoots up quickly from what some regard as the most fertile soil in the world. Most of the people are farm laborers, although the majority of them own no land.

Coming from the Philippines, I found the contrast immediately evident. I had been accustomed to a variety of landscapes, but now forest-covered mountains and cascading streams would be no more than a memory. It appeared to me that the terrain of my new home was almost uninterruptedly, monotonously flat. Markets along the highways seemed to be unvarying conglomerations of low tin sheds. Towns boasted slightly higher buildings, but nothing that would intimidate the most shy villager. I had arrived in winter, and the air was as pleasant as an autumn day in Indiana. There was no hint of the approaching swelter and sweat.

The Holy Cross Fathers and Brothers and Sisters had preceded us to Bangladesh by over a century. They had accomplished a good deal among the small Catholic community (2/10 of 1 percent of the population). Many Muslims gave them credit for their useful educational and health care institutions. From the ranks of Holy Cross, and from some of the diocesan clergy as well, we found affirmation for our intention to approach Muslims outside of parish structures.

Islam is the state religion of Bangladesh, as could be expected in a nation where six out of seven persons are Muslim. While Islam has always been the predominant religion, the proportion of its adherents has increased steadily over the years. It was our intention from the start to insert ourselves—in some way as yet unknown to us—into the neighborhoods and lives of those people. To live among Bangladeshi Muslims was a project for which there existed no job description. Heretofore the church had placed its personnel in parish houses, convents, and institutions. But no priests or brothers had set out to immerse themselves in the Islamic milieu, i.e., to draw water from the same pumps and to bathe in the same ponds as they did; to share everyday laughs and inconveniences with Muslim next-door neighbors. That was the objective in 1975; it remains so two decades later.

When I arrived in Bangladesh, I spent some time considering how to make myself most useful in service. I chose the sick and disabled as those with whom to involve myself. Attention to sick persons—especially the "hopeless" cases—would, in fact, alleviate the sufferings of only a tiny percentage of people. But, it would also give witness to Christian love for the most abandoned, and to respect for their lives. By living physically quite close to the poor I intended to make myself available to them in their medical needs, and also simply to show them that we *are* one.

As soon as I began to serve the sick, I was intrigued to see how different their perception of me was from my own perception of myself. Bengali Muslims, I soon learned, do not believe that any benefactor is purely so. That every helper expects a reward pretty well summarizes their attitude. If I were to live among the poor, offer necessary services to persons having serious health problems, and subsequently neither seek nor accept rewards of any sort from them, then perhaps I could help them to understand a form of love that they had not previously experienced, that is, the love of a stranger who seeks no recompense for the benefits he brings. In fact, that is how this apostolate took shape and developed.

In the beginning, having settled in Tangail district, I placed emphasis on serving as many of the sick-poor as possible in that locality. After nine years there, at a time when I was well acquainted with health facilities and doctors in the area and, therefore, able to offer competent assistance to many persons, the Spirit moved me to relocate—in order to offer the same witness elsewhere. Thus I moved to Kishorganj, a hundred miles away, to ease the pain of a few, and to explain to many others who asked me the reasons for my presence among them and my solicitude for the infirm. Witness, in other words, became as important as service. With the move in location came an accompanying shift in emphasis. Whereas extensive service to the infirm had been my priority, the witness to unselfish love in new communities now took on prominence. Henceforth, I wanted to move into new areas in order to live out signs of Christian discipleship on a broader scale for the full Islamic community: signs of hope for the poor, reconciliation between religious people, and equality of the poor with the rich.

About this book. I am not an author but, rather, a diarist. One would grasp the reason for that admission immediately upon entering the hut I call home. The floor is earthen and damp; the walls are thatched bamboo. There is no ceiling; a bamboo roof slopes up from a height of six feet to a peak at nine feet, then back again to six. For furnishings there is neither desk, typewriter, nor electric lamp. Even coffee, that vital provision for the writer's trade, is in short supply. A bed board and a backless stool fill a third of the hut. Whenever I write a letter—as I have to my parents every week during my thirty-one years in Asia—I seat myself on that stool and lean back lightly against the bamboo post by the doorway. (To lean back heavily or abruptly would contribute to loosening the post and weakening the frame of my hut.) Resting my elbow and forearm on the bed board I write in longhand. Usually, I finish before the funny bone in my elbow signals numbness or my feet begin to fall asleep. This arrangement for writing is awkward, impractical, nonconducive to extended periods of reflection, and ultimately fatiguing.

Still, the writing is important in holding onto the daily experiences of mission life. I do it, first, for my own benefit. It seems true to me that a person deeply knows only that which he or she is able, at least in part, to explain. Writing helps me to know what I am thinking. Second, I do it for others' sake. God has placed me in circumstances which few missioners are privileged to enjoy. I should record some of this. Someone may wish to review it and probe it.

Thus, as I bicycle here and there, I occasionally stop to jot down an idea or to note a connection that has occurred to me. That practice is not recommended during one's first months in a new locale in Bangladesh because onlookers—by whom one is always surrounded—take a dim view of strangers who go around writing notes. He feeds their fancies about the CIA. But there is no other way for me to preserve my thoughts than by scribbling urgently on the backs of scraps or used envelopes the ideas I hope to enlarge on when finally, at day's end, I can seat myself once more to record, from a spine-bending position, the frequently spellbinding experiences of one day in mission.

On Wednesday each week I accompany prospective patients to the regional hospital in Mymensingh. Before the doctors arrive I scurry to the bishop's house, open a typewriter, and transcribe my notes from the previous week. Then, at month's end, I gather the pages and forward the resultant journal from Bangladesh to Maryknoll and on to family members.

The rhythm of life is quite similar no matter where I live in Bangladesh. Thus, the experiences recorded in this book are not necessarily in chronological order, nor need they be, because what has happened in one place and time could just as easily have happened in another. However, the experiences are not commonplace. In fact, when I sum up these past twenty years in Bangladesh, the words *fascinating, illuminating,* and *stimulating* instantly come to my mind.

The invitation to transform these notes about a life in mission into a book was a welcome dare. I am aware that not every missioner feels or speaks about Muslims as I do. I hope they will record their experiences so that I can understand their reasons for responding to Muslims as they do. My customary experience of Muslims—for whatever it is worth—is positive. I admire many Bangladeshi Muslims for reasons which I hope this book will make clear. My prediction is for a future of improving relationships between Muslims and Christians. Moreover, I have reasons for the optimism and hope that I feel. The unity among peoples that Jesus prayed for is not, I think, in the dimly glimpsed future. In fact, I believe I hear whispers and see clues of realized oneness, here and now. Briefly stated, this Catholic Christian missioner-priest holds that Muslims are good.

To Robert Ellsberg, editor-in-chief of Orbis Books, for inviting and encouraging me; to Maryknoll and Maryknollers for enabling and befriending me; and to thousands of Abduls and Ayeshas of Bangladesh for inspiring and challenging me, I offer—as they say in Bangladesh—"Heavy thanks!"

Prologue

A New Town

This is the day I have been looking forward to, the day I will attempt to insert myself into a new town. The town I have chosen (a choice confirmed by the bishop) is Jamalpur, a rail junction on the Brahmaputra River, with a population of 101,000. My periodic transfers from one district town to another are in imitation of Jesus' approach to mission. Jesus, the compassionate stranger, moved from area to area and in every place paid special attention to the hopelessly infirm and to sick ones who had no relatives or friends to assist them. The crowds who witnessed Jesus' acts were gripped by his compassion, and not exclusively by his cures. Bengali Muslims are no less astounded to receive compassion from a stranger.

After Mass and breakfast, Bishop Francis wishes me godspeed. At the train station in Mymensingh there is some controversy about whether I can take my bicycle on the express train. Finally, a station man intervenes on my behalf: "He needs it. He is a friend of the poor."

Upon my arrival at Jamalpur Junction station one and a half hours later, a local *taut* [cheater] tries to extort money from me, but I refuse. He is willing to settle for a mere cup of tea, but I decline his help. The first order of business in any new town is to find a place to stay. Having already visited and reconnoitered the town, I know the places where I will not search for accommodation. Amidst brick houses and paved roads I do not care to live. Where television sets abound I quickly pass by. A neighborhood peopled by hawkers, rickshaw pullers, coolies, and other day laborers is the target of my search. Is there a vacant hut, or space to build one, in their midst? All I need is a place large enough to accommodate my sleeping mat, a kerosene stove, and a bicycle. The place must also be private enough for me to celebrate Mass and to pray every morning before it becomes light enough inside for curious ones to peer through holes in the walls.

I bike to a nearby rice mill where my contact, Golam Mustafa, works. His pals grill me for awhile. Then Golam and I leave to inspect his warehouse, the place where he has offered to let me live for a few weeks while I seek a permanent dwelling. However, upon seeing the condition of the place, I know at once that it is unsuitable for my needs. I suggest we try our luck at house-hunting near the train and bus stations on the south side of the town.

Some of Golam's friends have other suggestions, but nothing turns up. Kajol, a student, offers to help, but he can produce only a brick house. I politely demur. Ibrahim, a boy of nine, leads me to another rental. But when I learn that it is in a Hindu compound, I am relieved to discover that it is already occupied. I must live with Muslims. A young man named Amin shows me a new tin house available in his family's compound. It is too good for me. Next, he leads me deep into the neighborhood where we find an appropriate hut. However, the owner is adamantly opposed to allowing a single man to dwell in his compound, because there are teenaged girls around. This is a typical concern, and I take no offense.

At this point Amin has another idea and tells me to follow him. Inside his family's compound he points to the cooking shed. "You don't want anything *that* simple, do you?" he inquires. The shed stands about four yards from the family's house. It measures almost eight feet by ten. The walls are incomplete, made of bamboo and bits of old tin. The roof is bamboo over plastic sheeting. The floor is earthen and unlevel. There is a nearby tubewell, and a semi-enclosed latrine that doesn't flush well. I know at once that God has readied this place for me.

I meet Amin's mother, Jabeda. She requires 100 *takas* per month in rent (i.e., $2.70). The family seems solicitous and polite; four teenaged daughters and one son remain at home. Of course, I accept. Quickly I begin the necessary task of buying utensils and equipment. Cycling twice to hardware shops along the main street, I haggle for and buy a kerosene stove, a fuel jug, and a liter of kerosene; a large pot with a lid, a hurricane lamp and a sauce pan; a high-sided plate from which to eat rice, and a small jug from which to drink.

It is 7 P.M. by the time I finally get to cool off in a nearby pond. Amin and a dozen young men gather to watch me bathe, to stare at and interrogate me as I refresh my grimy self. The first item prepared on my new stove is a pot full of boiled water for drinking. Folks have never seen water boiled for drinking, and some gawk as I gulp the barely cooled fluid. Even greater surprises are in store for them, and for me, as we mutually observe one another.

Firoz Miah, the owner of the compound and father of this family, comes to see me at evening time. He is low keyed, pious, and kindly. His watch-repair business has been ruined by digital watches. A husky youth named Sharif invites himself into my hut. He tells me I am welcome to watch TV at his house any time; he also wants urgently to go to the U.S.A.

Visitors, including many of the neighborhood women, keep arriving until 8:30. They have many questions, wanting and needing to know who I am and why I have come. If these skeptical, curious, good people were to accept me unquestioningly from the first day of my stay, then what need would there be for my mission among them? They know no Christians, or certainly none who claim that following Jesus is the purpose of life. They know no missionaries, but they do know stories about the zeal of missionaries for conversions and the relentless efforts of missionaries to tempt and mislead faithful Muslims. I shall never grow weary of telling them that, although I am a Christian and will never be otherwise, I also recognize the good in Islam, that I wish for them to remain Muslim and holy, and that Muslims and Christians are intended by Allah to serve one another and cooperate with one another in service to the world. How could I ever grow tired of saying these truths to those who have never heard them expressed?

Finally, I eat some bread and turn in by 9 P.M. But rest does not come easily. As is usually the case when I enter a new town, it has been an exciting day. And yet the excitement is always mixed with a certain anxiety. Within hours I know whether the new town will be my open-armed home for the next three years or will instead be the place that spurns me. I really ought to trust God more and worry less. There has never been a town that turned me out. The Merciful One never fails.

PART I
Dialogue of Life

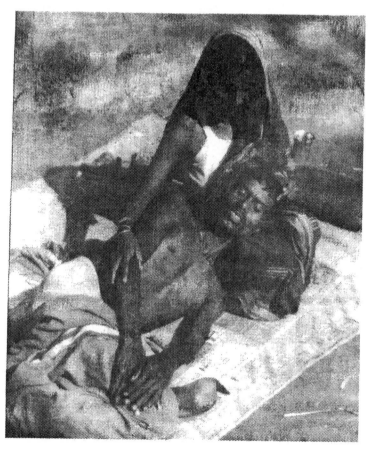

A farmer, exhausted and overcome with illness, lies outside his house while his wife comforts him.

The Model of Jesus

❖

At the beginning of 1975, I had no idea that before year's end I would be living in a new country, learning a new language, and setting out on a second career in mission. During the previous eleven years on Mindanao (an island in the Philippines) I had immensely enjoyed assignments to remote missions in Davao Oriental and Zamboanga del Norte. I loved the people and the physical challenges a missioner had to surmount in order to serve them well in their barrios. I envisioned staying there for life and made efforts to obtain citizenship. But then, unexpectedly, Maryknoll sought volunteers for a new mission in Bangladesh. The prospect of being able to work completely among Muslims was especially attractive to me, and I signed on.

The major reason which moved me to opt for Bangladesh was not, however, its Islamic complexion. Rather, the condition of the people and their country drew me strongly. Throughout the previous five years I had read reports of tidal waves, a war of independence, famine, cyclones, and floods which had mightily strained the people's endurance. I simply wanted to help them. That response was one I had learned from my mother and father: When someone is in trouble, try to help. Basic Christianity. I imagined that with so many folks in such hard straits, surely it would be possible to help a few. And I should, indeed, try to help, because I am a Christian. In such circumstances, what else would Jesus have his disciples do?

What else could Jesus have intended for us to understand by relating the story of the Good Samaritan?

Shortly after finishing language school, I was inserted—by God's direct intervention, it seems to me—into a district town named Tangail. I soon learned that the physical needs of the poor are colossal, that the people are open to receiving help for their health (although initially skeptical of the possibility that a stranger who offers assistance can be trusted), and that, therefore, it would be feasible to offer assistance to grievously ill persons who had no money, or who had no relatives courageous enough to joust with government doctors on their behalf. I decided to be their brother, to give them hope.

Simultaneously, another need became apparent, one which I could not have anticipated before reaching Bangladesh and meeting the people. They needed to experience altruism. They needed a taste of completely free, disinterested generosity. Habib, an educated man with whom I became close, told me frankly: "There are no disinterested persons. We know it is so. Everyone who gives has a condition to his gift. A person must pay for everything in one way or another." Some of the worst offenders in this category, he alleged, are Christian missionaries. They offer valuable assistance to the poor in matters of health or education. But behind their apparent compassion is a greedy motive. Missionaries want you to convert, to renounce your religious community and join the Christian religion. Missionaries help poor people, yes. But that is in order to win them to another religion. Self-interest is their real motive—surely not love.

Habib's words stung, for he was telling me how Muslims think of me. Whereas I had come to be useful to the poor and not to convert them, these people had been conditioned to perceive my motivation quite differently. There was no thought in my mind, or inclination, to exploit the people's poverty, using it as a means to more easily insert the Gospel message. I wanted only to spend my time, energy, and resources assisting as many as I could. But here was a warning: Expect to be suspect.

Nor was it possible for me to miss seeing that the poor of

Bangladesh already have a faith, one that I would soon learn bears rich spiritual fruits in their lives.

Nearly as revealing to me as the Muslims' suspicion of all missionaries was another fact related to money. Persons who received aid in kind or cash frequently belittled the aid, seeing it merely as a small part of a huge reservoir of money held by an international organization for distribution to the poor. An attitude of ingratitude resulted from their belief that the foreigner works for a large agency having untold sums of money, and that it is his or her job to dispense the help. No thanks are due to the worker; he is merely doing his duty. Believing that, it took no great leap of logic for some of the more aggressive people to make demands on missioners: You have received much money for the purpose of helping the poor. Give us what is intended for us.

From the first week of my twenty-year stay in this country I have observed that Bangladeshi Muslims presume to know more than they really do about Christian beliefs and Christian missionaries. In fact, although we often converse about values, they rarely ask what I believe about Jesus and about the purpose of missionary work. They imagine that they know all there is to know about Christian faith, that is, that Christians believe Jesus is Allah's son—an idea so repugnant to them that they can hardly utter it. The concept shocks them because they cannot abide the use of the word "son" in any but a literal way. Likewise, they do not doubt that they comprehend the purpose of every missionary's life. *Missionary* means *preacher* to them. To introduce oneself as a missionary, as I always do, is to Muslim ears an admission that one preaches in order to convert.

What, then, do Muslims question me about? Who are you? What are you doing here? they invariably inquire. I am glad for their curiosity, because it is the condition required for their learning something new about Christian belief and the missionary's role.

"My name is Brother Bob," I respond. "I go around looking for seriously sick people, that is, persons who are so poor that they do not even think of seeking professional treatment, and who lack the courage to go to government health facilities." When I find such persons, I offer to help them by accompanying them to hospitals. Such persons are not hard to find but, oftentimes, they have difficulty believing that a complete stranger is so interested in their welfare that he will spend time, energy, and—most amazing of all—a bit of money for their sakes. Perhaps one sick person out of five whom I approach will take the plunge required to go along with me. They are suspicious of people who claim to offer assistance for free. They are doubly suspicious when a missionary offers it, because they fully expect him—now or in the near future—to exert pressure on them to convert to Christianity. That suspicion is kept alive by neighbors and fellow villagers who remind the sick or disabled ones of the price they will have to pay in exchange for my assistance. I will, they convince them, press the sick ones to abandon Islam and embrace Christianity. I will, they warn them, be in a position to demand remuneration, and the currency I shall insist upon is their allegiance to my religion.

"My work is the same as Jesus' work was," I explain. "From the Bible we know that Jesus went about doing good to all and healing those who were grievously ill. That is why I do this work, because Jesus did it before me. Jesus is my model in life. I am trying to follow Jesus' example, just as you Muslims strive to follow the example of Mohammed the Prophet. Personal service to persons in need is an important part of my religion."

"Why do you think I want to convert you?" I sometimes ask persons who are most openly skeptical of my motives for assisting broken people. "Do you think I want you to become a Christian? I do not. I want you to be what you want to be. I want you to be the very person whom you think Allah wants you to be. You wish to be a good Muslim, no? I also wish that. You should try to be a good Muslim, and I should try to be a good Christian. Is it not so? I also believe that Hindus [who belong to a religion that many Muslim Bangladeshis despise as idolatrous] should be good Hindus and that Buddhists [whose religion is unknown and inconsequential to most Bangladeshis] should be good Buddhists. And we should all strive to respect one another. If we are religious people, we will respect one another. Who ever heard of a truly spiritual person who held other religions and their followers in contempt? Are we not all fellow creatures, created by Allah?"

"What will I receive if I become a Christian?" men ask me cynically. "Suffering" is my one-word reply. Even if a Muslim were to fake his acceptance of a new faith in order to gain material advantages, other Muslims would heckle him and make fun of his betrayal. His name would remain tainted by the stigma of having gone over to the traditional adversaries of Islam. Taken aback, one man presses his point, saying "I know that Christian missionaries give money, or houses, or cows, for anyone's conversion. I have heard it from reliable people!" "Brother," I reply, "even if you give me 100,000 *takas* [$2,500, i.e., more than ten times the per capita yearly income of Bangladeshis], I will not accept you into the Christian religion." It rocks them to hear it. They had been so certain that missionaries would go to great lengths to conquer Muslims and attach them to the Christian religion.

Unfortunately for the cause of mission in Bangladesh, it is true that some missionaries have used material goods to lure Muslims away from their religion. "Briefcase missionaries" is a term of derision used by Christians to describe the most recent wave of preachers, representing sects, who invade and convert, but generally eschew follow-up. Their one aim is, indeed, conversion—that is, the enrollment of other religionists on a roster. It matters little to briefcase missionaries whether their converts are from Islam, Hinduism, or from other Christian denominations. These missionaries can be compared to buyers, but not to maintenance personnel. Wherever such missionaries appear, bitterness abounds. Muslims despise what they perceive as the use of Western riches to mislead and subvert the simple faithful in Asia. Hindus clothe their contempt in rueful smiles. And Christians hate the tactic which further divides their tiny communities into new and smaller entities. The worst part, for mission, is that the reputation of such briefcase missionaries remains long after they depart. Indeed, their reputation attaches to other missionaries who have a decidedly different vision of mission. All missioners are viewed as guilty by association with the bribers.

Educated Muslims have heard of the Protestant Reformation. They know Christianity is divided. I try to put that into perspective. "I am a Catholic Christian missionary" I tell them. "A missionary is a servant of humankind. A Christian is a follower of Jesus. To be Catholic means that I belong to one of the two traditions within Christianity. The other tradition is Protestant. Just as you Muslims are divided into Sunni and Shia, so also we Christians are divided into Catholic and Protestant. As Sunnis and Shias are all equally Muslims, so Catholics and Protestants are all equally Christians. Our divisions are not made by God. Is it good for Catholics and Protestants, Sunnis and Shias to be separated? No, it is not good. But, that is the way things are. Our artificial divisions reveal a tendency within us to go our own ways, to divorce ourselves from others when we cannot easily reach agreement. Do we believe that God is one and that all of Allah's creation is one big family? Yes, we all do so believe. Yet, we are so blind of heart and weak of will that we suppose we glorify The One even as we reinforce our separateness. Mere mortals think small thoughts. Allah alone is great. Allah's will is for our oneness and togetherness. We must behave as brothers and sisters to all."

One of the questions put by Bangladeshis in order to help them determine a person's respectability has to do with education. "What is your qualification?" they want to know. I reply: "My best qualification is that I am a human being, just like you." They protest: "No, no, you do not understand. What I want to know is your educational qualification." When I admit to holding a master's degree in religious education, the inquirer is invariably surprised. Perhaps he is thinking: How could it be that this simply dressed, wiry old man, wearing sandals made from old automobile tires and a dusty cap, riding a beat-up bicycle and displaying one rolled-up pants leg—in order to avoid entanglement in the bike's greasy chain—is the holder of a master's degree? The Bangladeshi is sure that holders of such degrees dress nicely, ride motorized vehicles, and avoid activities which might soil them. I remind inquirers, again, of our common humanity. "Brother, my highest qualification is to be a human being. In Allah's eyes we are all absolutely equal. As for educational attainment, it is true that I spent twenty-one years in schools, colleges, and universities. But what good is education if it does not prepare a person to serve the needs of others? In fact, I believe that no one who is truly educated evades service to fellow creatures. Service to others is the mark of a genuinely educated person." Muslims' customary response to that proclamation of good news is a thoughtful nod. Normally, it so amazes a Muslim to hear an educated person claim radical equality between the literate and the illiterate that he maintains a stunned silence. The more educated he is, the more it astounds him. He knows well the Islamic teaching about equality. But to hear the teaching proclaimed by a disheveled degree holder gives new meaning to a familiar belief.

"What profit do you gain by helping others?" Muslims ask me. "The only profit I seek is Allah's *doa* [blessing]," I reply. "In Islam you have a beautiful saying: 'One who serves the poor serves Allah.' I believe that wholeheartedly! I serve the Creator by serving his [the Bangla language is gender-free; "his" is the same word as "her"] creatures. The Creator—the Most Generous One—rewards me now, with blessings, that is, happiness. The Creator will also reward with everlasting life all of us who serve one another. Do you not also believe that?" Most Muslims readily agree.

"We all desire to accomplish Allah's will for us, do we not?" I inquire. "Allah has given all of us special abilities and inclinations. To one he gives skill as a farmer. Thus, he plants and weeds and harvests with speed and dexterity. To another, Allah has given patience with children and cooking skills. Another can repair motors while yet another sews expertly. Into *my* heart Allah has placed compassion for the disabled and sick. When I assist them, I am certain Allah is pleased. When you do the tasks for which Allah has fitted you, then surely you please Allah, too. All of us are striving to do the will of Allah in ways that have been given to us. All that is good comes from Allah. We must, therefore, respect one another always. We should admire one another frequently. And we ought to praise one another—Muslims, Hindus, Christians—for all the goodness we see in one another. Brother, we are family! This I believe."

My stark avowal of our oneness usually induces a long, thoughtful silence. But there are others whom it challenges or provokes. They feel threatened by a Christian who speaks of unity between Christians and Muslims. It puts them on their guard. Nothing that they have heard or seen in their lives has prepared them to trust a Christian missionary. Such persons feel the need to publicly display their suspicion, to assert, through their responses, that they are not going to be taken in by this new evangelization. And so, they protest by harking back to themes that accent our enmities. These ancient arguments establish the superiority of Islam over Christianity and reinforce the need to keep distance between us.

Persons such as these, filled with suspicion, are probably the reason for a famous saying, "It is hard to do good in Bangladesh." I first heard this saying from a development officer who was working for a volunteer agency. He may have been referring to his experience of the factionalism in Bengali society which hinders cooperation among people within groups or villages. Or perhaps he was referring to a characteristic which Bengalis most frequently accuse themselves of: *hingsha* [envy]. People jest about the tragic consequences of envy; it inspires them to pull one another down. A missioner is confronted by the same reality, but he also faces an obstacle not endured by the development officer. There are always Muslims who are convinced that the missioner wants them to cease being Muslims. While nothing could be further from the truth, that suspicion is not easily overcome. But, praise be to Allah, it *can* be overcome.

In every one of the towns where I have lived alone among Muslims, each passing year has been marked by a characteristic change in the attitude of the local people toward me. Broadly speaking, the first year is distinguished by suspicion. Upon learning that I am a Christian missionary, people instantly suspect that my motive for coming among them is harmful—that is, to convert them from Islam. Those who are not threatened by my presence are at least mystified by it. Why would anyone choose to live in a bamboo hut among persons with whom he is unacquainted, having no other program than service to sick and disabled persons? Why would a foreigner offer service in such an inefficient way—using a bicycle instead of a motorcycle for outreach, and using kerosene instead of electricity at home?

The second year is marked by a growth in trust. The poor whom I assist are the first to trust. They do not require much explanation about my identity and purpose. They quickly sense that I am *for* them and that my intention is wholly benevolent. They see proof of the missioner's sympathy for them in the use he makes of his aging body. When I go around on a bicycle searching for persons most in need of physical healing, they perceive an able-bodied old man who seems eager to toil for their welfare. I accompany them to hospitals; some I even carry there. People who are healthy—especially those who are educated members of the middle class—discuss among themselves the sight they see. They ask me: "What is in this for you?" Happiness now and an eternal reward, I reply. Faith-filled, pious Muslims approach and tell me: "Although Islam is the best religion, no Muslim would ever inconvenience himself for others the way you do."

During the third year I can feel an increase in their affection for me. By then I am nearly everybody's "uncle," or, to some few, *abba* ("father"). Adults acknowledge me in public places, children greet me with "Good morning!" in every part of the town. Young men shout a friendly "Bob Brother!" and some of them, perhaps referring to my riding habits, hail me with a loud "Young man!" Curious men cease to interrogate me distrustfully and begin to question me calmly, as if to signal that they are no longer interested in proving that the claims of my Christian religion are false but, rather, that they wish to understand better the reasons for my way of life and obvious concern for neglected persons. Mothers hand me their children to hug and to bless and, occasionally, to name. "Does your family not miss you?" adults inquire. "Who will bury you and weep for you if you die in this faraway place?" I reply that my family has sent me here and that they pray and sacrifice financially for all of us living in Bangladesh. As for death, I propose that nobody ever dies. Muslims, Hindus, Buddhists, and Christians—all shall live forever.

This, roughly, is the pattern that is duplicated every three years in a new location. There are, of course, persons who trust the missioner from the very start. For them there is no first step of suspicion. On the other hand, there are some whose suspicion of missioners never ceases. They are stuck in their biases. However, as a practical rule, Muslims who observe the missioner living in the thick of their everyday lives are struck first by suspicion, then by trust, and finally by affection.

Thus have I concluded significant stays in four district towns. But my connection with every locality has not been terminated; in fact, it remains strong through periodic visits. At least twice a year I return to Tangail—where I lived for nine years, until 1986—and to Kishorganj, my home from 1986 until 1989. I pay even more frequent visits to Netrakona and Jamalpur, my homes from 1989 until 1992, and from 1992 until 1995. The people in the four towns are accustomed to seeing me return. I have overheard surprised Muslims ask one another "Why did he come back? Will he live here again?" Another replies correctly: "No. He simply wants to see his friends again." In this manner, over a period of time, friendships mature, acquaintances become warmer, and horizons expand. Onlookers become well-wishers as they grow accustomed to the notion that it *is* possible for Christian to respect Muslim, light-skinned to be concerned for dark-skinned, and educated to serve unlettered. The term "missionary," with its negative connotations, takes on a new meaning.

Life among the Poor

❖

On most days I awaken at 4:00 A.M. without the help of an alarm clock. I slide out from under the mosquito net, refasten the *loongi* (an ankle-length wraparound worn by most Bangladeshi men) around my waist, and then squat to light the hurricane lamp. The same match is put to ten wicks on the single-burner kerosene stove. After pouring a cup of water into the sauce pan for heating, I measure out a spoonful of instant coffee in a cup. I sip at the coffee for five or ten minutes before snuffing the lamp and assuming a position of prayer—once again, under the mosquito net. With my back against a bamboo post, legs crossed in lotus fashion and hands resting in my lap, I pass an hour with the Lord. Throughout the time I simply wait on God without book or beads in hand. Time passes peacefully; this "wasting time on God" is the most reassuring exercise of the day. *Father . . . Lord . . . Thou . . . Come . . . One . . . Am . . .* These are an assortment of mantras, but I use them only occasionally. Most often the prayer time passes without words but with much awareness of God.

By 5:30 light arises in the east but the interior of the hut remains in darkness. Again I light the hurricane lamp, put up the mosquito net, and reach into my small tin trunk for Mass equipment. Having arranged it on the bed board, I position myself as before for prayer and commence the celebration at which I am reader, server, offerer of intentions, and congregation. On such occasions, approximately

350 times per year (Holy Week and Christmas are spent with Christian communities, elsewhere), I substitute silent reflection for the homily. I celebrate Mass in the Bengali language, careful to keep my voice ever so low because my nearest neighbors live one yard away and their curiosity is easily aroused.

When the Mass is completed, I extinguish the lamp and prepare to face the day.

❖

Inside my hut I sit writing. All my attention is focused on the pad of paper upon my knee. Vaguely I am aware of someone coming in through the doorway. A small, naked body approaches. The six-year-old boy thrusts his hand directly into the path of my vision and holds it there rigidly. Not a word is spoken. Distractedly I take the proffered paw. The silent one initiates the shake. Then he zips outdoors and rejoins his sister on the pathway toward the river where he will bathe. Handshaking fever (i.e., the need to shake my hand) continues to afflict all the little boys and even some of the daring girls in this neighborhood.

Handshaking is not the normal way for Muslims to greet one another. Frequently they use the hand for a kind of salute, but seldom for shaking hands. Handshaking is a custom they have learned from outsiders. In general, I am glad they have learned it. The atmosphere in this neighborhood gets cheerier every time a smiling child offers me his hand, or demands to press mine. Still, there are times when I wish they would desist. Raju, for instance, is a four-year-old neighbor who has the habit of waiting until I have mounted on my bicycle before he runs to my side to collect his handshake. He wants my right hand no matter how much I may need it to stabilize the vehicle. When three or four of them catch me on the bike, it becomes a test of my skill to touch every one of them without losing momentum. These children may be the reason for my epitaph: Bob Brother, Christian missioner, who died from an excess of handshaking with Muslims.

A woman pumps water from the communal tubewell.

Abdullah is four years old, black, fatherless, swollen with edema, and dying of tuberculosis. He is so weak that he must be carried everywhere. I had told his twenty-four-year-old widowed mother to meet me at the government TB Clinic. After she received a free, one month's supply of medicine from the clinic for her only son, I gave her four duck eggs—my prescription for his good health. Abdullah's eyes bulged with expectation when he saw the eggs; his mother smiled sweetly, showing her betel-stained teeth. As I bade them goodbye, the boy whispered urgently to his mother: "Bananas!" She conveyed his request. I just happened to have four of the fruits in my bag. Abdullah counts me among his friends because of it.

That was six weeks ago. Today, a woman hiding her face within her *sharee* motions for me to stop. "Abdullah, your friend, is dead," she announces. The boy's mother recalls how much the child enjoyed the eggs and bananas he had received earlier. At that time she and I both hoped to be able to arrest his pulmonary tuberculosis. But we were too late and now Abdullah (the servant of Allah) is with Allah. "Abdullah's eight-year-old only sister is coughing now," she adds in a monotone. She knows now what we can expect even if we begin the treatment. It may not work. It may be too late. A lifetime of eating too little, too seldom, cannot be reversed by mere medicine. A diet rich in proteins, and plenteous, is just as essential for her cure. A widowed mother cannot afford special food. She feels fortunate when the owners of the kitchen she works in give her a kilogram of raw rice so that she can fill her family's stomachs. A healthy diet, in her estimation, means that their tummies are comfortably full. It may be a mercy that she lacks knowledge of the value of proteins, for such foods (lentils, eggs, meat, fish), though available, can be purchased only with cash. She does not receive cash for her labor; raw rice is her wage. That is why tuberculosis usually kills the poor who contract it. That is why it is not enough to know about a balanced diet. One must also have the means to purchase it. All sorts of rich, health-giving fruits and vegetables,

meat, fish, and grains are available in thousands of bazaars throughout Bangladesh. But Abdullah's mother and millions like her do
not even bother to go there. Without cash, what's the use?

My closest neighbors were rather excited that a jackal had forced
its way into my hut while I was gone. What excited me even more
was the invasion of ants. The whole south side was piled with ant
hills, and red ants—which have a fierce bite—were scurrying to secure
their fortifications. As Alim passed by, he advised me to sprinkle
with kerosene the one hundred or more holes the ants had bur-
rowed. I did so. Another neighbor, Jinnat, counseled spreading ashes
from the hearth of her kitchen. Soon she reappeared, accompanied
by her two daughters and lugging a pan of hot ashes for dislodging
the intruders. With neighbors like these, we shall overcome.

It seems to me that we are really good neighbors when we exchange services with each other the way we do. I serve their sick
ones. They readily share with me their expertise on house maintenance. My service is based on knowledge of where to go and whom
to see with patients. Their service is founded on the practical knowledge that comes from having lived in flimsy shelters for a lifetime.
Each one gives; all benefit. We are a functioning part of a mystical
body composed of Muslims and a Christian.

Every now and then as I bicycle toward town, Monoara, a young
mother, sees me approaching and leaves her hut to intercept me.
She usually has a white patch pasted to each of her temples—a local
treatment for the headaches from which she frequently suffers. Today she has to hustle to reach the road in time. As I pass by I hear a
shout: "Brother!" Glancing sideways, I behold the *sharee*-clad lady
running full tilt down the path and waving energetically. A narrow
canal runs along the side of the road; she broad-jumps it as smartly

as any boy before skidding to a stop at my side. "Monoara, what's on your mind?" I ask. "Do you remember the little vitamins you gave me once?" she pants. "You must give me more of them, because I am always exhausted." I don't ask why.

There is so much to sap the strength of a Bengali woman. The Bengali diet is heavy on carbohydrates, especially rice, and light on proteins—eggs, fish, meat, and green vegetables. Although the women do the cooking, they are the last ones in the family to eat, and sometimes not much is left for them. The heat that oppresses everyone is extra hard on grown women because they must wear the *sharee*, a head-to-toe covering, and particularly because blouses fit so tightly under the arms that profuse sweating is unavoidable. Whatever other daily chores they do, they must always pound spices, haul pots of water, keep track of children, and frequently bear new ones. Crowded conditions make privacy minimal; they urgently need to take a break, but seldom do. If only they could get away from it all for a while, to reinvigorate.

Toward the end of the morning prayer-time, an ornery six-year-old boy rattled my bamboo door in order to rouse my ire. Stepping outside quickly, I caught the little tease and twisted his ear. Only then did I notice two young mothers standing with their children, waiting to see me. When they observed my mood, one of them, Hamida, faded away. Some hours later she returned to see me.

"What is it, Hamida?" I asked.

"While you were away," she began, "my youngest daughter died." I fastened my attention on Hamida as she unfolded the entire saga of Sorufa's last day, how her breathing became labored, what she said to her mother, and how she did a little dance while delirious. Hamida had been waiting to tell me that story for more than a week.

While Hamida spoke, tears ran down her cheek. I shared her pain. Occasionally, as she whispered her story, I managed to repeat

Allah's name. I felt ashamed that I had not attended to her earlier. She had carried within her the wrenching story, waiting for me to bear it with her. All she wanted from me was compassion.

In Bangladesh there are many like Hamida for whom we can do nothing better than to give our undivided attention. We share a common vision of life and death with them. They sense that we respect life as precious and hope in the life to come. When someone dies, we easily overcome the caution that characterizes our inter-faith relationships. Why, then, should we not hurdle the wall that separates us, in order to behave throughout our lives as brothers and sisters?

Most of all, I was struck by Hamida's kindness in coming back when I was fit to listen. How typical of the Bengali woman to wait patiently for the right moment to reveal what weighs heaviest on her heart.

There is nothing like a quarrel to wake up a neighborhood. The faithful who have been fasting stir slowly at 7:00 A.M. Others sit drowsily in their huts rubbing weariness out of their eyes. In front of a small store, two men exchange radically opposed views, voices at full volume. (Quarrels are more common in the month of Ramzan than at other times, it seems to me. People are more easily irritated when their eating habits are disrupted.) Soon fifty persons have gathered around the two men to seriously attend to their mutual grievances. Others in the vicinity have heard the ruckus and scurry to the scene; mothers tote their suckling babies.

In some societies, people avert their gaze from quarrelers, to save the opponents from embarrassment after they have cooled down. In Bangladesh, however, people hasten to participate in quarrels as spectators and jury, for the opponents need an audience with whom to share their pique and rage. If witnesses were to hold themselves aloof from neighborhood flare-ups, there would be nothing left for the quarrelers to do but to start swatting each other.

Violence does occur in Bangladesh, of course. But, more often than not, the path of compromise is followed. My clearly perceived impression is that—given the poverty, heat, crowdedness, and provocation with which people are confronted—physical violence is rather limited. People do explode, but it results in noise more often than mayhem.

I had devoted a whole day to helping Anoara find work. Several days earlier I had spoken with a tailor who was planning to start a sewing class. He had pledged to enroll Anoara, free of cost. Anoara badly needs employment to support her three children. Halim, her husband, has a mental problem and his support is quite irregular. She was full of enthusiasm for this chance to learn sewing by machine.

On the appointed day, Anoara walked from her village in time to begin the 9:00 A.M. class. The tailoring instructor had said he would arrive by 10:00, but he arrived, instead, at 1:00 P.M. After a brief conversation with his pupil, he broke the news to her that the design and cloth-cutting part of the course could be followed only by literate persons. Anoara neither reads nor writes. She waited in the classroom for a while, watching the other young women as they started the course that would enable them to earn money. Then she left to walk the five miles home, and to ponder her rejection.

Anoara is an intelligent person who never got the opportunity to study. The sewing course will last for four months, but for Anoara it ended at 4:00 P.M.

Chewing the betel nut is a passion for many in Bangladesh. For fifty *paisa* (about one U.S. cent) people can enjoy a flavorful, hunger-repressing, breath-sweetening treat. The fragments of betel nut are wrapped inside a soft leaf and sprinkled with an assortment of exotic spices. Chewing the concoction also strengthens people's jaw muscles, so much so that regular chewers are as noteworthy for powerful jaws as they are for reddened tongues and blackened teeth. Betel stalls are found everywhere, and vendors hawk the product on trains and boats. Most vendors assemble a single wad at one time, but recently we passengers witnessed a master betel hawker in action. Twentyish, cheerful and loquacious, he fascinated an entire train car of weary travelers with his enthusiastic patter as he put together ten wads simultaneously. The number of spices and scents he added to the ten succulent leaves was four times the usual. The listeners were enchanted, and vied to buy these creations, even though they were selling for double the normal price. Such panache in a betel vendor is rare. Betel vendors do not have to be original or ambitious for sales because so many persons want their product. This vendor demonstrates what showmanship can do for sales in Bangladesh.

As evening fell, Halima was sweeping the earthen passage that separates our huts, and grumbling. "I don't have a single *taka* to buy kerosene for our little lamp." I called to her, and as I filled her lamp with kerosene from my jug she related how Jabbar, her husband, had been taken by a friend. "My husband gave him 1,950 *takas* ($49) because the friend had promised to repay it quickly. But now he won't repay it. My husband trusted him because the man wears a prayer cap and says his prayers regularly." Raton, Nizma, Golenor, and I listened sadly and exchanged knowing glances.

I spoke for all of us when I suggested, "Halima, we cannot judge a person's trustworthiness by his clothes or his public prayers. Only a person's behavior, observed over a long period, tells us whether or not someone is worthy of our trust."

Then Golenor spoke up: "You can trust a person if she or he does good for others. We can trust Brother," she stated, looking my way. "I tell people we have a *feresta* [angel] living with us. He spends money on sick people who are complete strangers to him."

I tried to deflect her praise by a play on words. "You have a *feringi* [foreigner] living with you, not a *feresta*." But no one laughed. They do not like to think of me as a foreigner, even though that's what I am.

Just before turning in for the evening, I was sitting outside in the dark with six or eight family members. They asked about Mom and Dad and my other close relatives. Ratna, aged twelve, piped up to say, "Uncle, when you die, we will bury you here; is it all right?" Raton, her father, motioned to hush her, but I told him she had put a good question, and offered a good solution, too. Death is a topic Bangladeshi Muslims see no need to avoid. Death is part of life. Indeed, Ratna, do bury me where my hut is.

"I am here; do come in," Kamola beckoned me when I arrived at her hut. On entering I saw a scene that should have given me unalloyed joy. Kamola was sitting on a wooden bedstand cradling in her arms twins, forty hours old. After having lost all of her past six children during their infancy, she is delighted to be a mother again, but quite concerned for her children's future.

A few weeks later the three were living in a leaky house when rain drove them out. A neighbor let them stay for the night in his crowded but dry quarters. Then Kamola, unable to see any alternative, walked to where her husband and his second wife live. Kamola is not very welcome there, but she is not seeking niceties; just a dry corner in which to nurse her babies will suffice. I offered to photograph the three of them there and, after I had, Kamola asked me about the boy: "Is he sick?" I looked at the boy and frowned. "I think he's hungry," I answered. "I have not got enough breast milk for both the babies," she explained. "Please bring me some powdered milk for the weak one."

Weeks later I approached a craftsman as he sat cross-legged in his tiny stall waiting for customers. He makes wooden frames for photos while you wait. We agreed on five *takas* per frame, and then he started sawing the soft wood. As he inserted a 3" by 5" photo into the completed frame he gazed on Kamola and her babies. "Twins" he stated. "They will never make it" he continued, "because when the poor have twins they both die." As a matter of fact, one already has.

I saw a parable today. Patients were arriving on foot and by rickshaw at the local hospital. Out of one rickshaw stepped a man whose ailment must have been internal, because there was no sign of affliction on his body. As he paid his fare, my attention was drawn to the rickshaw puller's condition. Hanging under his chin and protruding forward and sideways from his throat was a goiter half the size of his head. He pumps that three-wheeler and ferries those passengers ten hours a day, three hundred and fifty days per year, in order to put rice in the family cooking pot. He has no time to stop in order to attend to his own physical problem. That is typical of Bangladeshis, especially married ones.

I've heard it said that the best cure for self-absorption is service to others. Among the parents of this country I observe little self-absorption. They are responsible—and feel that responsibility—for the stomachs of their children. Featured weekly in an Asian magazine is a table that illustrates the average caloric intake per day for people in fifty nations, worldwide. Consistently, the first and last places on that list are occupied by the United States, with 3,671 calories, and Bangladesh, with 2,021 calories. The major nutritional problem for Bangladeshis is not that the markets lack foodstuffs. There is always food for sale, and most of the time it is reasonably priced. The problem is that the poor do not have enough cash to buy a sufficient amount of food. And, now that there are more than 120 million people crowding this Iowa-sized nation, it is not at all uncommon for adult women and men to weigh in well under 100 pounds.

A barefoot widow has brought her four-year-old son, Mashood, to the dingy emergency room of the local hospital. Hours later I see them in the ward. Mashood's broken leg is in traction. The widow is in her early thirties and has eight children: five girls, three boys. Her husband, Ali Akbar, died ten months ago in the very ward where she is now staying. Since her husband's death she has been living with her father-in-law in the village of Nagan. But it is a difficult life. "He keeps telling my children to go away. What am I to do?" She gets misty-eyed when she tries to explain how she is going to make ends meet. I assure her of help for the boy's present problem. That relieves her mind a bit and opens her to conversing with me. The only times she has ever visited the town have been on the two occasions when she has had to come to the hospital. Thus, the town holds no appeal for her; it is the place one goes whenever disaster strikes. She wants only to be at home with her children. I do not know her name, but I recognize her heroism.

Among the men in this district town who beg full-time for a living, one afflicted fellow had never approached me. Then, today, as I walked east and he was stumbling and staggering west, we crossed paths on a deserted side street. It was then I learned that this twenty-five-year-old man is not only crippled in the right arm and leg, but also mute. We faced one another. He grunted, took my hand and held it against his bare, flat, empty stomach. We made our way slowly to a nearby restaurant. I inquired if they would let him enter the premises. Permission is required. Many are the restaurants where shabby persons may not be seated or served, no matter how much money they have. The owner nodded assent. The mute one entered as quickly as he could. Once he seated himself I poured water over his right hand. The table boy had barely finished adding lentils to the plate of rice when the mute plunged his hand into the plate, melded lentils into one fistful, and stuffed it into his mouth. He ate greedily with full concentration on the plate before him. It is not easy for a mute to explain to people how very hungry he is.

It occurs to me that besides the psychological wound that this disabled mute must bear—because he lives on the street and is totally dependent on whether people choose to notice him or not—begging is basically hard physical work.

A sickly woman came to me today and I hope that we shall be able to help her get well. What is your name? I asked her. "Bilal's ma" she replied.

There is a place in the world where numerous people do not know their own names. That place is Bangladesh. All of these unself-conscious persons, in my experience, are Muslim women. They appear to have normal intelligence but severely restricted experience. That is, the village boundaries are the limits of their physical world. People refer to these women by their oldest son's name. He may be Arif Miah; she is known as Arif's mother. Their identity is so dependent upon the sons they have borne and nurtured that they have been absorbed into their offsprings' identity. I have met hundreds of these good, simple women. Their inability to tell me their own names never fails to jolt me. Probably I shall never get over this reaction to them. They are among the truly poor. They do not even demand to be known apart from the children they have borne. Their humility is beyond my reach.

I was rushing to catch a bus. As I reached the bus stop, I noticed a man wearing a sleeveless knit sweater sitting on the pavement.

Blood oozed from his nose and mouth. It puzzled me that so many people, sitting or passing close by, ignored him. The bus arrived and departed without me. I knew the Lord was calling me to stay with the stricken man.

"What happened?" I asked him. He looked at me for a moment. His eyes told me he knew he was critically ill, but he showed no panic. Nor did he speak to me. A rickshaw was parked slightly ahead of us. Its puller/driver glanced at the man and turned away. The man in the sweater had been his passenger; they were on the way to the hospital but they had not made it. The man in the sweater began to bleed more profusely. Thick, dark red blood pushed out from his nostrils and from between his closed lips. Suddenly, surprisingly, he got up and retreated from the street to the open doorway of a hardware store. Quickly he removed the sweater, smoothly pulling it over his head without smearing much blood. Why or for whom are you saving that sweater? I asked myself. Is that the inheritance you are leaving for a son if your family ever finds you? Or are you simply too warm on this winter day?

Putting the garment aside, he propped himself against the wall. The betel nut stall-keeper and his customer were trying not to look at the drama six feet away. I moved toward the rickshaw puller to learn what he might know, but he was on the verge of vomiting and unable to answer me.

The sweaterless man pointed toward a water pail. A cup attached to a cord hung beside it. I ripped the cup free, drew water and handed it to him. With a steady hand he put the cup to his lips. After one small gulp he set down the cup and leaned his head back. Blood burst forth. The hardware store owner, taking momentary notice, gruffly ordered the rickshaw puller to unfold the man's legs so that he might die in the correct position. The man's eyes, so clear and alert until the end, finally shut.

The puller looked around for someone, anyone, to help him. "This foreigner doesn't know how to help," he muttered. He was right; I did not know what else to do. I stood with hands upturned to Allah for my unknown Muslim brother.

Over the next few days, the image of this man in the sweater remained with me. How does a thirty-five-year-old man, hemorrhaging uncontrollably on a city street, far from loved ones, so alone, embrace the end so calmly if God be not with him?

A young mother with three children had learned of my need for a short piece of bamboo and volunteered to bring one from her house. Not only did she bring the bamboo, she also fetched a hacking knife and cut the bamboo down to the exact size I needed. The task took her ten minutes. Afterwards I presented her with some leafy vegetables and a phial of iron tablets. They are strength givers. With my thumb I had pulled down the skin beneath her right eye, and had observed that the underside of her eye socket was white from anemia. Nevertheless, she carries on, as if energy were not needed in order to initiate such kindnesses as hers.

The following day, my "house repairer" returned. Perhaps she felt that she had labored too little in exchange for the gifts of vegetables and vitamins. Upon seeing me she immediately announced, "Your shirt is dirty. I will wash it for you." I was taken aback and about to deny that I wear dirty clothes, but before I could formulate an excuse she grabbed the short sleeve on my left arm and taught me how to recognize dirt. About that topic she is an authority. Like most Bengali women, she spends time each day of her life at the riverside or at the tubewell, pounding the dirt out of her family's clothing. The following day I wore a shirt that had never been cleaner.

The menacing sound of whooshing wind and the fervent prayers of my neighbor in the next hut awakened me from a deep sleep. Quickly I got out from under the mosquito net, groped for matches, failed twice to light the hurricane lamp, but finally succeeded during a momentary lull in the storm. Following a pattern I have learned,

I unlocked the door to my hut and pulled on my trousers. If the roof gets carried away (I told myself), I at least want to be able to exit through the doorway. And, with the prospect of hutlessness in mind, the minimum I can do is dress for the great outdoors. Then I yanked my thin mattress away from the bamboo wall where it was being splattered by rain. The time was 10:10 P.M. I passed fifty minutes reading the *Bombay Examiner*, praying, and listening to the heartfelt entreaties of Shahab Ali, my neighbor, to spare his family and his home. By 11:00 the wild winds had passed and only a slight rain continued. Wiping water off the wooden bedstand, I again spread the mattress—but this time folded it in half so I could sleep on the dry portion—lowered the net, and turned in. At 6:00 A.M. I went outside to throw away shaving water. There stood Shahab in the midst of the dwelling that used to stand beside mine, caressing the one good piece of bamboo that remained. Looking my way, with a blank facial expression and an emotionless voice, he summarized the storm of April 24: "Our house fell down."

Nature can wreak havoc in any nation, advanced or not. But I know of no place where more people per square mile fit the description "at the mercy of the elements" than the Bengal. Throughout history, cyclones have funneled up through the Bay of Bengal and smashed into the southern coast. Flood waters descending from the Himalayas in the north have immersed the river-crossed nation during monsoons, and tornadoes have ripped it up with impunity. The same hothouse environment that makes this one of the lushest countries on earth also ruins buildings of historical importance. In fact, many structures would be historical treasures had not heat, humidity, and wind conspired to rot them before their time. The storm that felled Shahab's house was a mere windstorm. It is among the least of nature's punishments in Bangladesh.

Anyone who has worked closely with Bengalis has observed a striking trait. It is this: Bengalis appreciate and value whatever they

Bengali children—curious, bold, playful—make every neighborhood lively.

receive from another as the result of having requested it themselves. For example, I may spontaneously volunteer to shoot a photograph of a Bengali who is not expecting the favor. That person has a hard time understanding why I did it. More than likely, that person suspects me because of my kindness. "What does this fellow want from me?" he or she asks. On the other hand, if that same person were to approach me to request or demand a photo, my compliance would give him or her great satisfaction. If I were to begin by refusing that request, but later give in to further hectoring for the prize, the consolation would be supreme. This characteristic of the Bengali is, for missioners of all faiths, worth pondering. As for proselytizers, they are suspect persons. One who pushes and strives to persuade is not to be taken seriously for his message. Anything a Bengali really wants she or he is willing to pester another person to give. If the Bengali does not request, demand, hector, or pester a prospective benefactor, then the benefactor might just as well hold on to the object in question. In this culture, spiritual and material gifts are truly appreciated only by those who ask, seek, and knock. Moreover, the more they perceive that the prize came to them because of their own perseverance in knocking, seeking, and asking, the more genuinely they will value it.

Two eight-year-old boys are standing in the middle of the street and making political speeches. They are pretty good mimics of the histrionics of real-life politicians. Shuwel (a holy terror whose mother, at her wits' end, has been known to predict she will someday throttle him) is promising in bombastic fashion to bring peace to this neighborhood. The other fellow, whose name I do not know but who is recognizable by missing front teeth and short pants through which his bottom is plainly visible, is pledging jobs for all who vote for his party. The two are shouting at full throat; hundreds of people can hear them. No one thinks it unusual for boys to mock politicians by exaggerating their styles. The fact that Shuwel is standing on a peace platform is ironic. Wherever he goes he shatters peace.

A wiry, emaciated elderly woman carrying scraps of wood in a basket was returning to her village after spending the day scavenging. She put down her loaded basket and descended to the river to wash away the sweat and grime of her hot and dusty work. After immersing herself, she began to rinse and wring out her coarse green *sharee*, section by section, while it clung to her body. I had nearly finished bathing when she, smiling sweetly, said to me: "I have not soaped this *sharee* in weeks. If I had a bit of your soap, I could wash it properly." The ball of soap I had brought was only one-third of its original size. I handed it to the woman as I passed beside her on the way home. Her blessing followed me. "You will be rewarded by Allah, but only in the next life." Soon afterwards, she placed the basket on her head and set out for her village home, wearing the sopping wet piece of cloth which is the only garment she owns.

To be requested to share by a person who cannot afford to buy soap for bathing or laundering is a privilege. To be reminded by one who struggles every day merely to survive that a reward awaits us, in heaven, is to live in the best and healthiest earthly environment. To be blessed by a woman who is so poor that she has no change of clothing is evangelical joy.

"Bob Brother" . . . (pause) . . . "Bob Brother" . . . I did not respond. Malaka, the eight-year-old girl standing in the doorway of my hut, could see I was concentrating on a book. For months I have been trying to get the children to respect my privacy while I read, write, or eat. If the matter were left up to them, they would look inside, see me, greet me loudly, insist on shaking my hand or shoot questions at me, such as: "What did you eat most recently?" My failure to respond to children when I am busy is quite in keeping with the Bengali custom that when people do or say things that you would rather not see or hear, you simply ignore them. Ignoring others is viewed not as an act of arrogance, but rather, in most cases, as a form of self-defense.

Before arriving in Bangladesh, I had never experienced a culture in which ignoring persons is such acceptable behavior. Some persons, by means of ignoring others, succeed in evading unpleasant distractions. So, Malaka waited until I finished reading the page and then beckoned again: "Bob Brother?" "What is it, Malaka?" I replied with satisfaction, happy that I was being instrumental in teaching her to wait while her elders are busy. "Bob Brother, your house is burning," she informed me with concern in her voice. Sure enough, behind the kerosene stove, the bamboo wall was disintegrating in a slow, flameless burn. Ignoring the persons who would speak to you may be justified and practical in some instances, but in others it can be costly.

One of the best children's pacifiers in all of Bangladesh is the lowly biscuit. Every neighborhood store stocks them. Packed in cellophane by local companies, biscuits are inexpensive and hugely popular. Oftentimes a child will hold on to one without even nibbling at it, simply beholding the good fortune that is in his hand or basking in the joy of possession. An equal number of children eat them quickly, as if holding onto the biscuit would burn a hole in their hands. No Bengali child I have ever seen would turn up her or his nose at a biscuit, even though, it seems to me, biscuits have little flavor. In children's terms, biscuits are considered wealth: children prefer biscuits to clothes, games, or hugs.

A one-year-old girl sitting securely on her eight-year-old sister's hip offered me her biscuit today. What a kick I get out of children who are already trained to share their precious biscuits. This wee lass actually extended her treasure toward me, placed it in my hand, and let go of it. She was not faking her generosity. Nor was it a matter of giving away one cookie and then replacing it with another from the cupboard. There are few cupboards in rural Bangladesh. A package of biscuits, once opened, is soon gone. If you receive a biscuit, consider yourself happy. But eat it within a few minutes, lest you notice someone admiring it; that could move you to give it away.

All the vehicles going to and coming from the town were delayed for an hour at a place several miles from here where a boy, aged ten, had been run down on the narrow highway by a speeding bus. The corpse could not be removed from the road. Until the police or the stricken one's family arrived to take the body away, no other person would have dared to take on that responsibility. A crowd gathered quietly. How revealing are the facial expressions of Bengali women, men, and children when confronted with a gory death. There were no pained, pinched faces or squinting eyes. Calm, thoughtful viewing characterized the whole crowd.

Once I was called to the house of a dying man but, by the time I arrived, he had expired. Loud lamentation ensued. His wife was grieving audibly. A small, naked child stood at her side without comprehending the reason for the commotion. A relative took the child by the arm and led him close to the dead man. "Your father is dead; look at your father," the relative directed.

There is little effort wasted in protecting youngsters from the unpretty sights of destruction and death. The attitude seems to be: Let the children see it; ravages are a part of life. Moreover, if everything that happens is traceable to Allah's will, then no human condition should repulse us. Life begins, continues, and ends. Why should we behold the first and middle stages but shrink from viewing the final one?

Mirza dropped by to see me today and to announce the happy news that Dolena, his wife of one and a half years, had given birth to their first child yesterday. Virtually all Bengalis hope for sons, especially in the case of a first child. Mirza, however, had not conformed to the customary in that respect. He had been hoping for a girl, and had already picked a name for her: Kathy, after my one and only sister, of whom Mirza had seen photographs. In fact, during the final few months of Dolena's pregnancy, whenever someone had something to say to Mirza about his wife, they referred to her as "Kathy's mother." Mirza had let it be known that this first child, if a girl, would bear the name of a friend's sister.

One of the truths that Mirza's example illustrates is the facility with which educated Bengali Muslims embrace new views. Surely Mirza, because of his village upbringing, had been prepared to prefer a boy child. But he had listened to campaigners for women's rights, and the things he had heard from them and read made sense to him. One of the clearest indications of women's negligible status in Bangladesh is the almost universal desire among Muslims to have male children. A reversal of that attitude, therefore, would begin with the willingness to have female children. In this instance, the "affirmative action" approach is for a Muslim parent to pray to Allah for a daughter. That is what Mirza did. Not only is Mirza a righteous Muslim, he also wishes to lend his support and good will to the advancement of women in his culture and in society.

Alas, Dolena delivered him a son.

I am often amazed by the casual meetings I have with gravely ill persons. Many of them introduce themselves by saying that they have heard of me from other people and they know they can expect to receive effective help for their deteriorating condition merely by approaching me and requesting help. Yet, most of them do not request help until coincidence finally brings the needy into contact with me. They know, they say, that I am anxious to help. But they just never got around to seeing me.

Why would poor persons who are quite ill hesitate to approach a person who they have heard is sympathetic, has helped others who are afflicted, and will surely help anyone who needs hospital care? Possibly it is because they do not believe the part about "he will surely help you." They have little experience of altruism in their lives. Other non-relatives who have helped them have required repayment in cash, in kind, or in services. Their experience of receiving help is that it is part of a tit-for-tat exchange. If they feel they have nothing that I would want to get from them, it might dissuade them from approaching me. Another possibility is that the poor have never actively sought professional treatment for their ills. They do not put much stock in medical practitioners because they need their money for other uses. Spending on health is a low priority.

It may also be that casual encounters are regarded by the poor as the best encounters. That is, if we just happen to meet, then they believe that it was arranged by Allah. I once told some villagers that my bicycle route would henceforth no longer bring me to their village, but that I would still frequent a close-by village every Saturday morning. A woman retorted: "If you do not come to this village anymore, then there is no chance I'll go to another village to see you, no matter how great is my need!" Thus thinks the villager.

Mojibur, a youth of fifteen years, had to come home from the hospital. The doctors had told his father that they could not help his cancer. I saw the house he came home to. It is a little stick hut loaned to the family because Mojibur's hut is under water these days. Today, Mojibur, his father, and his uncle spent four hours in a rickshaw coming home. No one travels that far in a rickshaw unless they are desperate. Mojibur was exhausted by the trip and panted for air. His right thigh was huge, frog-like. People gathered around the rickshaw when it came to a halt. One youth said clearly, in Mojibur's presence, "He will not live." He was not being cruel. It was, rather, a direct statement of what he knew to be true. At least, Mojibur did reach home. The most terrible thing would have been to die away from home. Worse still would have been to be buried far from his family. So all are satisfied that the three reached home while the boy still lives.

Mojibur likes sugar biscuits, so I bought him a large packet. As I started to leave, he took my hand and begged my pardon. Imagine: A teenager is dying, suffering intensely as he awaits death, and he seeks my forgiveness. For what? Because I had gone to a bit of expense for his cure and he had not cooperated by getting well? Or because I had paid for the rickshaw fare and would not be receiving anything of personal usefulness in return? That would not be the case, of course. Mojibur's example is quite useful to me. Allah has already given me forty years more than Mojibur will get, and I must remain grateful.

In the village of Ramdevpur a sick young mother had not been much helped by advice I had given her earlier. I now promised Jelimon that I would pray for her. "Yes, do pray for me," she echoed. As I started to leave she held up her hand, a gesture to make me stop and listen. In a weak voice she thanked me for something else I had done for her, the value of which I had not realized at the time. "I'm just so happy that you showed me the photograph of your father and your mother. She is so pretty."

My family has supported me financially ever since I arrived in Bangladesh. But their most practical gift to this sick woman is that photo, taken thousands of miles away and fifteen years ago, which has served to invite Jelimon into their lives.

The children in Norshinghapur village are usually a bit wild when I visit each Saturday. The village is across the river and roadless.

Most outsiders who appear are walking through, toward other villages; bicyclists are a novelty. Today the kids got too rowdy. Dozens of small children grabbing at my moving bike, hoping to unseat me, tried my patience. As I was leaving the village, several older children pursued me with screams and laughter. Then one of them threw a clod that struck my spine. Swiftly I dismounted, laid the bike on the trail, shed my slippers, and dashed about 100 yards before running down my terrified assailant. I pushed him to the ground and walked away. A couple of parents were taking all of this in, so I approached them. The older of the two was already reprimanding the children. I complained: "I just don't understand. Every week I come here to see whoever is sick and to be helpful to them. Why can't the children simply let me pass by in peace?" Nazim enlightened me with this explanation: "They say you are *pagol* [crazy]." This kind of crazy person is not really insane but, rather, crazy for Allah. The term refers to a person who is heedless of all things but Allah. Nazim told me this seriously, confident that his explanation would help me understand the reason behind the children's unruliness. Indeed, it did that, although some might say that he merely added insult to injury.

There is in this part of the world a tradition of withdrawing from ordinary occupations in order to follow a different drummer. Not many people are *pagol*, or become *fakirs* [mendicants], but many of the Sufi-influenced Muslims of Bangladesh respect this tradition. The asceticism of the *fakirs* and others like them involves being at the mercy of whoever wishes to share food or shelter. A *fakir* or a *pagol* does not care much for anything. He puts up willingly with foolishness and abuse because his heart is not set on receiving the respect of his fellows. He wishes to be—or to appear to be—so lost in the Transcendent One that the treatment meted out to him by others is irrelevant to his peace of mind. He is a person you can pull pranks on, safely. On the other hand, I belong to a faith having saints who are known to be fools for Christ. They joyfully bear opprobrium and suffering because the perfect Model for living did so. Unfortunately, I am not one of that sort.

I arrived unexpectedly at the hut of Toyob Ali. Within five minutes the elder of his two married daughters had sliced up a pair of mangoes and presented them to me in the family's one and only dish. The whole family lives in three huts constructed of mud and straw; their huts are not surrounded by the traditional fence. They do not have enough money to buy the inexpensive, dried sticks of jute needed to construct a rudimentary wall. Not one of the members of this family wears sandals. They even had to borrow from a neighbor a weak wooden stool on which to seat me. And yet they made my day.

The mango is not only the most delicious fruit in Bangladesh, it is also the most expensive. Naturally, it impressed me to receive the fruit of kings in the home of the poor. However, the true measure of this family's hospitality was evident when they responded wholeheartedly to my unexpected arrival. The essence of the spirit of hospitality, it seems to me, is seen in their decisively dropping their own little projects and spontaneously offering full attention to the unexpected one. What a charism. It is a charism that I do not claim to possess. When I see this sort of hospitality enacted toward me or toward others, it humbles me. What a grace it is to regard those who come to you as having been sent by Allah, and to respond in accordance with that belief.

Somsher Ali is a man sixty years of age who walks with a stick and wobbles. He trudged five miles to see me today, and I was amazed that he *could* walk that far. I gave him some eye medicines as prescribed by a doctor at a free eye clinic. Later, I saw Somsher bumping his way through hundreds of shoppers in the vegetable bazaar and invited him to join me for a meal. He plopped down heavily in the chair and, although I was sure he had to be hungry, he accepted only a small plateful of rice. He expects blessings in small doses from the Merciful One. He hopes for nothing more from life than what he has received, and he takes whatever Allah sends—the good and the bad—as if there were no other way that things could have happened. A book could be written about his life; it would be immensely instructive for the monied and the powerful if they chose to pick it up, read between the lines, and meditate on it. But no book will be written because he is simply one of millions in the same circumstances. His working life is long finished. His property was sold to pay the dowry of a daughter and medical expenses for his wife until she died. He has no relatives capable of supporting another mouth, no matter how modest his appetite is. Meanwhile, he stumbles around, realizing that he looks pathetic but not caring. He feels driven to survive, but accepts that his life will be over on the day when he can no longer walk into town to beg.

Above the driver's seat of a bus I rode not long ago were two thought-provoking and practical statements, inscribed in bold black letters for the attention of literate passengers: "At the time of crossing the river on the ferry boat, passengers will get down from the bus." Beside that good advice was this: "While sitting in your seat be thinking of Allah." The instruction to get off the bus before it moves onto the ferry has been ignored often—and at great cost to life. (Occasionally a bus will miss the ramp and plummet into the water, where the bus becomes the passengers' coffin.) The second counsel is the one that intrigues me. In how many countries of the world would one find public transportation vehicles prominently featuring spiritual encouragement? Indeed, in some countries a written reminder to pray or to be mindful of the Creator would be studiously avoided because it would be seen as bad advertising. Transport operators in those places would not want to shake the passengers' confidence with statements about the Owner of Life. But Bangladeshis are realistic. Buses are dangerous to ride; accidents happen frequently. Recognizing this, transport owners perform a further service to the public by urging people to keep the Almighty in mind while they travel, for Allah is the Best Protector.

Two young women came to my door this afternoon. Rezia carried her three-year-old son on her hip. This young mother, probably about twenty years old, has had two children. Because her husband wanted it, she volunteered for a tubal ligation. Soon after the operation, one of her two children became sick and died. Thus, a great deal of her future welfare is riding on the son she carries on her hip. Rezia's husband only occasionally can secure a rented rickshaw by which to earn a daily wage. His irregularity of income forces her to work in the home of a neighborhood "big man." In exchange for her labor she receives a cup of tea and a piece of bread each morning, one new *sharee* each year, and 40 *takas* in cash per month. She will become old before her time.

Accompanying her was Ayesha, a quite pretty eighteen-year-old. She has no children, having lost two of them late in her pregnancies. As her husband has no regular employment, she works in the large house of a historically prominent family of the town. Her pay also is 40 *takas* per month. Breakfast and the yearly *sharee* may begin later; it depends on whether or not the family likes her work and allows her to continue it. It is difficult for anyone from my part of the world to fathom how any person can wear herself out for the equivalent of $1.35 a month. Ayesha chews betel nut and the habit results in visibly strong jaw muscles. When she bites down, the sinews streak plainly between the corners of her mouth and the curvature of her jaw. Her lower face has become prominent from overexercise. Chewing betel nut detracts from her beauty. However, it also reduces her hunger pangs. Looks do not count for much when a person is hungry.

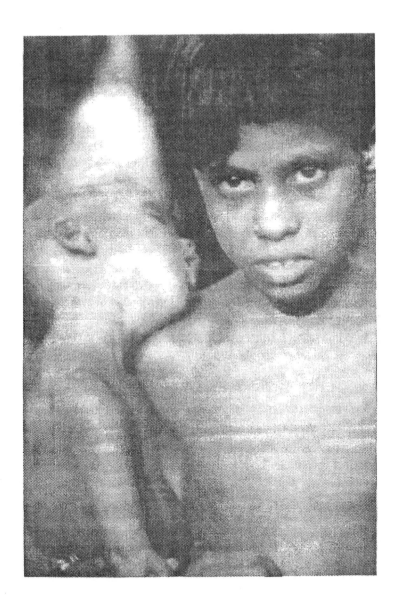

The barber I frequent is in a buoyant mood today. He is elated and grateful that his five-year-old son is alive. He had taken his sons, ages 7 and 5, along with him to the river when he went for the daily bathing of the family cow. As the barber washed the cow, the boys splashed around nearby. Suddenly the older boy called to his father: "Abba! Little brother is gone!" Frantically the father lurched and probed in the muddy waters. All was in vain. Then, as he was about to go crazy from frenzied grief, the little guy's body popped up out of the water. His father hauled him to the river bank where he did a crude sort of resuscitation. Behold: the child responded. Now the boy is at home and normal. "My son is well, by your blessing," the immensely relieved father tells me. "You must come to my house to eat *sinni* [an inexpensive sweet] with us, to celebrate my son's return." I assure the barber he is already doing much for me by trimming my mustache, and that I already share with him the joy and gratitude that he feels. "I will pray for you and your family in thanksgiving to Allah," I offer. He beams his approval. I have not seen a happier man in weeks.

Sweet potato season falls this year, helpfully, during the month of fasting. As they are inexpensive, filling, and tasty, sweet potatoes make an ideal treat for *iftar* [the snack with which Muslims break their daily fast] among the poor. This afternoon I gave a kilogram bagful of the uncooked tubers to Golenor along with the request that she boil the contents, for them and for me, tomorrow. She understood my intention and agreed to it. Two hours later she came to my door bearing a plate loaded with steaming hot sweet potatoes. Though she had consented to prepare them tomorrow, she also knows that it is nearly impossible to keep food overnight when there are hungry children around. I should have understood that immediately when, as soon as I handed the bag over to her, Yusaf, her eight-year-old grandson, snatched a potato and ate it raw.

Every once in a while an incident such as that one occurs, reminding me how different are the lives of people in the countries I know best. It happened again today, two days before Christmas, while visions of fruit cake danced through my head. I had given a few small potatoes to my neighbor and her daughter, Resma. Soon after that I was at the tubewell preparing to bathe when Resma approached and asked me to wash a single potato. I did so, although I did not understand what the rush was; her mother would not start cooking for at least another hour. When I handed the rinsed potato back to her, she immediately began to gnaw on it—raw. I would not have guessed that the little girl was so hungry. Hunger had been the cause of the rush. People here do not complain, not even the children.

On another occasion I brought home okra from the bazaar, enough to share with neighbors. I placed some of the vegetables on Rabia's bedstand while no one was looking. A moment later Rabia approached me briskly, smiling broadly and chomping on a piece of raw okra. I cautioned her that I had not cleaned the vegetable before giving it to her. "I am too hungry to wait," she admitted with a laugh. But she was serious. She explained that she had not yet eaten today; it was 4:00 P.M. How could anyone have known that she was running on an empty tank? Rabia was carrying out her chores, as usual. I had not even suspected her hunger. It is really hard to be aware of people's daily struggles because they gripe so little.

Early in the afternoon as I returned to my hut I found the atmosphere of the neighborhood charged with emotion. A death had occurred in the hut of our nearest neighbors. About twenty persons were actively commiserating with the survivors. "Haroon died one hour ago," a boy informed me. Haroon had been barely one week old. Walking closer, I saw the baby's mother prostrate on the ground and gasping. Two other women had flung themselves beside her and were wailing inconsolably. The baby's father was crying openly. There had been no warning of the infant's approaching death. Fever, such as Haroon had, is common at all ages in Bangladesh. I had held Haroon three times during his short life, and already I, like others, referred to him as my *bondhu* [friend]. Even though the neighborhood is already replete with children, Haroon will be sorely missed. His parents had been childless during ten years of marriage until he lit up their lives. The grieving now taking place is partly for the child who died before having received all the affection that people were anxious to give him. It is also for the tremendous loss felt by Haroon's mother and father and the extended family.

As the annual celebration of Korbani Eid approaches, Bangladeshi Muslims show special signs of respect for their elders, benefactors, and spiritual guides. Late this afternoon, on the eve of Eid, five out of the eight children of this compound rushed toward me, fell on their knees, and then bent their bodies until their foreheads rested on my feet. To someone seeing this for the first time it might appear that they were groveling. In fact, they were seeking a blessing, for this is a culture in which blessings are deeply appreciated.

On another occasion, I had just returned home after a three-week absence. Toward evening, when most of the family was at home and the novelty of my presence had worn off, I distributed gifts to everyone. That, too, is a custom among Bengalis. Crayons and notebooks were handed over to eight children, *loongis* were given to three men, and "maxies" were presented to five women. It was risky giving maxie house robes, I thought, because there are no other women in this neighborhood who wear that garb. However, the women were delighted and donned them quickly. When they came to show me how the long, billowing clothes fit them, each one stooped down to touch my feet. Nazma, the young woman whose hearing and speech are impaired, had been sick and moping around until that moment. Her transformation was sudden and happy. She pointed toward Allah's paradise and held her hands in a position of praying. Then, gracefully, she pointed toward me with an open hand to extend her blessing.

I often marvel at the patience of Golenor for Nazma, her deaf and dumb twenty-five-year-old last child. But today Nazma was sobbing when I returned to my hut. She had received a plateful of rice from her mother and, for some reason, had thrown it aside. Golenor was so upset that she beat Nazma. I stopped at the hut where Nazma was sobbing. Welts had risen on her arms and back; her lower lip was puffed out. Golenor sat in the doorway, glumly staring out. She told me matter-of-factly what she had done to Nazma. She was far from being proud of it. In fact, I could tell that she was sorry; but she had to punish one who wasted food. The use of food is a serious matter in Bangladesh. The abuse of it is like a desecration.

The next day Golenor got sick with fever and lay down all day long. The beating had deflated her. That evening, Nazma came to my door. "Ma, ma, ma," she stammered, using the only syllable she is able to pronounce, and pointing toward her prostrate mother. Nazma was crying tears of sadness for her mother's illness and withdrawal. Not long after seeing her daughter's tears of forgiveness, Golenor arose and began to go about her many works once more. Nazma's forgiveness had healed her.

Jahanara, my nearly blind, widowed neighbor, was lugging a bagful of something when I passed her on the road which leads to our area. I stopped to greet her and to ask if I could take the heavy bag the rest of the way home for her. She was pleased to allow it. Later she told me: "People say that you are good. You do not despise the poor." Whether it is so or not, the poor perceive that they are despised because of their poverty, the very condition over which they feel they have so little control. Jahanara reminded me of something I learned fifteen years ago from a friend named Mirza. "The Bengali people think that foreigners abuse women and liquor and that they despise the poor." Wherever that belief may have come from, the fact is that, until people here get to know me, they will have that preconceived view of me. According to the accepted wisdom, I, a foreigner, am regarded as an abusive person. No wonder, then, that Jahanara thinks it is noteworthy that I show the most ordinary sort of kindness toward her.

Oajid, a day laborer who lived 60 yards west of me, died three months ago. I missed the chance to console his family because I was out of town and did not return until the next day. In Bangladesh, burial follows so quickly after death that I am often surprised to learn, weeks or even months after the event, that someone died while I was absent for a day. This afternoon I thought to visit Oajid's family. His widow was kneading dough for a meal of bread. Their hut has no window, so smoke from the earthen stove was irritating her eyes, making her teary. Three children were sitting on the family's only piece of furniture, a wooden cot, watching and waiting anxiously for their share of the one-course meal. A fourth and tinier tot sat naked on the cool, hardened earth floor. It surprised me that the widow has children so young, for she looks older than she is. I was glad that it was raining. Perhaps that would allow me to visit the family without other curious persons coming over to learn why I was there. I wanted to give the widow a fifty *takas* note (worth $1.25). That is what I would have put on the offering plate beside the head of the deceased, had I been there for his burial. "This will be the first food the children have eaten today," the widow told me about the pound of dough under her palms. The three older children were smiling, perhaps in anticipation of tasty food, or perhaps because I was visiting them. "Oh, come on now," I joshed. "They ate *something* this morning, did they not?" The oldest girl—tall, skinny and pretty—gave me a look that confirmed her mother's statement. This would be the day's first bite. Amazing that these good people suffer in such silence, I told myself. It is good I was not here to contribute money when Oajid died, for they needed the help even more today. If all my training and efforts to come abroad had given me only today's opportunity to help this widow, I thought, it would have been worth it.

Nizam's mother has come to live with us. She shuffled into our compound a few days back, clutching the stick that is her cane and carrying no other possessions. She had come to stay. The old woman speaks little and appears to be weary. Yet, she reacted with vigor when a boy passed through our compound complaining of a sprained arm and bawling from pain. She summoned him to her, ordered him to hold out his arm, and told the boy to blow on it while she implored Allah's favor. After the boy finished blowing, she dismissed him without waiting to investigate the effectiveness of her cure. She has full confidence that the invocation of the All-Powerful One will solve the boy's problem.

At night Nizam's mother beds down on the east side of his hut in a cramped, barely enclosed space. Golenor, good daughter-in-law that she is, puts out a rough blanket for her. At 7:30 P.M. I saw the old woman lay down and then heard her begin singing to Allah in a croaky voice. She reminds me of Kathy, my sister, who used to sing herself to sleep in her crib. At about 8:00 someone placed a small plate of rice beside her. She propped herself on one elbow to eat it slowly. Nizam tells me that his mother used to live directly in front of where my hut now stands. "But then Abdul [his son] got married and had to have that space." That was ten years ago. His mother, a widow for these past three years, goes from house to house among her sons, receiving shelter. "We are five living sons," the sixty-year-old Nizam informed me, "and one daughter. Most of us have died. My mother had nineteen children," he says with pride. Nizam claims that his mother is ninety-five years old, and that is not out of the realm of possibility.

A rickshaw puller called me to a halt as I rode north by bicycle. We stood beside the road to discuss his son and wife who are in the hospital. Meanwhile, two seven-year-olds—a boy and a girl who are unknown to us—interrupted their journey to observe us. They each balanced a large basketful of grass and debris on their heads. Perhaps they had been on their way to feed the family's cow. Silently and attentively they waited for the two men to finish conversing. As I mounted my bicycle to depart, the boy wished me "Good morning!" When I returned the greeting, the girl wished me another "Good morning!" The children had patiently borne their loads and stood there, simply looking forward to the moment when they could offer me a greeting in perfect English. While I do not hanker to have people stop and listen in on my conversations, I do commend the children for their perseverance and gentility. And for their thoughtfulness. For they imagine that I love my language as much as they love theirs, and that nothing thrills me more than to hear a salute to the day in my mother tongue.

Most people know that engines cannot run without fuel and that guns do not fire without ammunition. There are some people, though, who don't understand that cameras need to be loaded with film. That is the lesson I learned today from Khatun, a thirteen-year-old neighbor girl. "Uncle, will you take my *photuk* [photograph]?" she wheedled. "Sure," I teased her in return, "I'll take it if you will bring me a roll of film. I have a camera, yes; but there is no film inside." Half an hour later she returned and stood smiling at my door, her appearance transformed by a layer of makeup and a new orange *sharee.* My mouth fell open. I did not wish to disappoint the teenager, but she must have misunderstood me. So, I carefully reiterated the need for film. She disappeared for five minutes, but then returned with half a dozen young ladies every bit as lovely as herself. This time, her mother came along too. I tried mightily to explain to the mature woman how her daughter's mistake had misled the whole band of stunningly adorned young ladies. But, even Mother appeared to be mystified by my footdragging. Her attitude was: "You admit you have a camera, and then you raise the separate and unrelated topic of film. Now, look! The girls are all dolled up for a photo. So, just take the picture!"

In the capital city, 110 miles south of here, people are becoming familiar with the principles of fax machines and computers. They have long since understood the basics of photography. But we live in a district town.

As darkness fell the children were seized by an urge to stage a program. A wooden stool was quickly put in place for me, the chief guest and entire audience. All the rest of the children who had gathered around were participating artists. No sooner had I sat down than Shiuli launched into a limerick she had memorized at school. The parents in this neighborhood, it seems to me, appreciate schools in proportion to the amount of verse the teachers can cram into their children's heads. Kakuli could hardly wait for her sister to finish so that she, also, could recite. Not, however, before Yusuf had inserted his song along with dance. Ratna, the oldest, followed with a short presentation of the proper English greetings for morning, noon, and night. Then Rina in her thin voice presented a poem. Resma, signaled by another child, shyly recited a short piece. It is not her style to volunteer. Labhlu, her brother—who is far from shy—offered a piece so long that one of the four mothers dragged him off "the stage," i.e., the small, vacant area in the midst of our assembly. He came back anyway, not to be deprived of attention.

They all wanted to show their ability to perform and to entertain. This went on while Rubel was tossing in my lap and grabbing for my spectacles. By the time our spontaneous program had ended we had spent thirty lively minutes together. Mothers were pleased that their children's memories had held up. Fathers were proud of this display of cultural richness amidst the physical poverty of their lives.

Nizam's mother does little else than pray her *tasbih*, that is, the Islamic "rosary." Whether she is sitting inside her lean-to or outdoors under a small tree, she invariably is running the large white beads through her fingers and reciting the ninety-nine beautiful names of Allah. When she is not using her *tasbih* she drapes it around her neck. She wears it like jewelry, but it is far more precious to her than gold. No contemplative nun or devoted Christian ever spent more time "telling her beads" than Nizam's mother spends with her beloved chain of piety.

Today, after her bath, the old woman suddenly realized that she had become separated from her *tasbih*. She grew agitated. Lifting her voice as high as it would go, she protested. In her panic she shouted, so that all of us could hear her contempt for whoever had made off with it. During the next ten minutes various children searched, but the beads were nowhere to be found. Then a granddaughter brought her *tasbih* from a neighbor's house, gave it to the woman, and told her frankly that another of her granddaughters had taken it. There was no reason given. The old woman's stormy emotions subsided as soon as she began to recite the beads once more. A new *tasbih* can be purchased for ten *takas* (25 U.S. cents), but to people like this pious woman, an old *tasbih* is priceless and irreplaceable.

A partial description of me might include the following characteristics: suffers foolishness poorly, answers back as good as he receives, and is not easily intimidated. Looking at me now and hearing those words a person could assume that I am simply a crusty foreigner in my mid-fifties living in the midst of a typical Bengali neighborhood.

The Bengali Muslims among whom I have lived in four towns during these past nineteen years surely see that side of me. They could hardly miss it. But they see something else, too. That became clear to me one day on a bus ride when an educated man from the first town in which I had lived recalled my days among them, saying: "People say you are an angel." I started to laugh at that, but checked myself when I sensed he was not kidding. On another occasion, a man from the second town in which I had lived summarized the perception of some of his townmates, stating: "They call you an angel."

What these people seem to have seen with greatest clarity and force was not so much my temperament but the witness of compassion I gave. Despite my impatience and testiness, the fact they dwell on in their minds is that I really did try to help people recover their health—people whom no one else was assisting, about whom none cared. They perceive that I did it as an angel would, that is to say, solely because it is holy to help people in need without asking for or expecting anything in return.

Both the men, interestingly, expressed their feelings long after I had departed from their towns. It makes me think that, if one wishes angelic work—love—to be instructive, then one should keep moving from place to place. It gives the people a chance to reflect on what they have seen.

This is one more example that illustrates a truth about Bengalis. They pay attention to what you do more than to what you say. Eloquence and oratory are second nature to them. But works that speak to their hearts are treasured for their rarity.

During these past few days people have come to see me at the wrong times, barged into my hut without knocking, asked for assurances that no human can give them, and not been satisfied until I have explained over and over again what we can try to do for a sick person's health. My temper has never been sweet; as I age, my patience wears thinner; the heat gets to me; I get a bit difficult. One could imagine that people's appreciation of me is diminishing as a consequence of my failures at gentility.

This morning, as I conversed with him in his home, the tuberculosis doctor made an uncharacteristic personal remark: "The people hold you in affection." Well, if they do it is because they have selective memories. Bengalis are great ones for ignoring what a person says and judging one on the basis of what one does for them and with them.

PART II

Mission and Dialogue

The Model of Gandhi

❖

One day, as I searched a dusty bookshelf for something that could hold my interest, I happened upon a booklet by Mahatma Gandhi entitled "The Message of Jesus Christ." Reading it made my heart glow. In it, Gandhi more than confirmed my belief that for the people of Bangladesh, where I live, deeds of love and respectful presence among them are the most important gifts I have to offer. Gandhi convinced me that these God-fearing people love their own faiths as much as I love mine. His example showed me that an intelligent, courageous, and exceptionally open-minded person, who is also deeply knowledgeable about Jesus, Christianity, and Christians, can and should remain a part of the faith that nourishes him or her. Although Gandhi gave prolonged and prayerful consideration to becoming a Christian, Christianity simply did not compel his belief. Not from stubbornness, but from grace, I imagine, he renewed his devotion to the faith into which he was born. In that way, Gandhi reinforced my feelings of friendship for the faithful of other traditions and respect for the faiths they love. At the same time, Gandhi proposed for me an incarnated approach to these good people, by way of service and simplicity of life among them.

I had only recently come to Bangladesh after having spent eleven years as a missioner in the Philippines when I happened upon the booklet. In the Philippines, I had tried to witness to God's love for the poor by spending myself as a teacher and a preacher, by giving spiritual seminars in the barrios of Mindanao, by offering Masses and administering sacraments among the good people who practiced folk Catholicism. Now, in Bangladesh, I was searching for a new mode of witness. Gandhi's input was timely and pivotal for my understanding of the witness I am called to give among Muslims and Hindus in Bangladesh. His words assured me that among the people of Bangladesh the witness of good works and sacrifice for others that springs from the love of God would have an unrivaled impact upon the hearts of the persons served.

In general, the attitude toward Christian missioners on the part of both Muslims and Hindus in Bangladesh is similar. That is, both are skeptical and suspicious. However, Hindus feel less threatened by missioners than do Muslims because their religion can absorb other points of view more easily. The expectation of both Muslims and Hindus is that missionaries come among them to snare converts. In view of that expectation, their tolerance for Christian missionaries is, on the whole, edifying.

Bangladeshis seldom ask me about my beliefs. Both Muslims and Hindus have strong, positive ideas about Jesus. They have learned of him from their own Islamic and Hindu teachers. They think they know what Christians believe, so there is no need to inquire. What they do ask, insistently, is "Who are you?" and "What are you doing here?"

I explain: "I am your Brother Bob, a Catholic Christian missionary. I am here to serve seriously sick persons who are poor. Service to the needy and love for all persons is my purpose in life. Christians believe that Allah makes happy those who serve the needy." To some others, I say: "This Christian wishes you well. I appreciate your faith and your culture. There is nothing about you that I seek to change except that which you also wish changed," that is, ill health in exchange for good. To still others, I say: "I am your Christian brother. I am a missionary, that is, a servant of all God's people. Jesus went about doing good and healing because he loved God, and anyone who truly loves God also loves other people. I follow Jesus. I wish to help the widow, the orphan, and persons afflicted in any grievous way. Your religion and mine both teach that those who serve the poor serve Allah. I respect your Islamic faith. It is good. My Christian faith is also good. You fulfill your faith; I'll fulfill mine. We shall meet again in Paradise."

When it is the police who question me about my purpose for living in a town where there are no Christians, I hand them a copy of the letter of assignment given to me by Bishop Francis. He states five priorities: "Live among the poor as a brother to them. Serve the sick so that they may live. Show the respect which our Christian religion has for Islam and Hinduism. Explain to those who inquire about the reason for your lifestyle and good works. Contact the Christians in the area (a scattered few) and encourage them to live good lives."

In a crowded neighborhood named Islampur, I live in a hut made of bamboo, like the homes of my neighbors. In this 13- by 7-foot room, covered by a low tin roof, I pray, cook twice daily, rest, and store my bicycle. The hut has no electric current. Water is available only at a nearby tubewell, shared with many, as is the toilet. "Why don't you live in a house that has an overhead fan?" sympathetic people ask me daily during the hottest months. They like to hear me repeat: "When you can do it, then so will I." They appreciate that the bicycle is used for their benefit, and that it makes possible the seeking and finding of disabled persons in many distant villages and bazaars.

I draw encouragement from the Good News for this apostolate. Spend yourself (Matthew 20:28), serve others (John 13:15), go and heal (Acts 10:38), practice your religion openly (James 1:27), and expect rewards from God alone (Luke 14:14). I draw inspiration also from Gandhi's counsel, adapted to these people and to this time: "A life of service and uttermost simplicity is the best preaching."

The people of Bangladesh have a name for the sort of service that expects nothing in return. They call it disinterested. They believe that it is either rare or nonexistent. Thus, they look for hidden, selfish motives in the good works of every missioner. They do not trust missioners. It is a lesson they learned from their colonial history. They perceive that missionaries speak of salvation while secretly seeking the conquest of those who follow Islam or Hinduism. The missioner is after something: our conversion. Genuine altruism does not exist in the missioner's heart. He has an angle.

In one sense, missioners have been a stumbling block to mutual respect among Muslims, Hindus, and Christians. Some missioners have, indeed, offered service to the people for the purpose of bringing them into a church. Muslims and Hindus do not regard such service as noble, for it aims at procuring a reward, that is, the conversion of Muslims and Hindus to Christianity. Such efforts are regarded by them as no more worthy of admiration than the attempts of a salesperson to sell a product that no one wants. Bangladeshis have told me: "There are no disinterested persons." Gandhi observed that the use of education and health care as a means for attracting Muslims and Hindus to the Christian faith is proof for them that missionaries are as selfish and self-interested as anyone else.

It is the spirit of disinterested love, illustrated by acts of mercy on behalf of afflicted persons, that touches the hearts of the Muslims of Bangladesh. Their response to compassion convinces me that nothing affects them more deeply than this disinterested, and therefore totally unexpected, concern shown by a Christian toward Muslims. Genuine altruism astounds them. "What you are doing for our people is very good!" they tell me. "Don't you know that people stay up nights talking about the fact that you wear sandals and not shoes, ride a push-bike and not an automobile?" As one laborer dramatically put it to his companions: "This man practices Islam better than we do!" Positive feedback of this kind reaches me from time to time.

Missioners in Bangladesh serve the purpose of Christianity better by disinterested service to the poor than by proselytizing them. It was Gandhi's view, and it is mine. Our services are determined by the people's needs. The poor among whom I live feel the need for an intermediary when they are seriously ill. Without such a helper, they will not often seek medical attention, even though government health institutions exist in virtually every locality to assist them. I invite the sick ones to those hospitals and clinics and accompany them to the doctors. The ailing ones regard my assistance as crucial. That no reward is solicited for helping them and accompanying them causes them to reconsider their idea of Christian missionaries. In addition to those who are sick, those who merely witness disinterested service—that is, people who are educated and those who are not poor—pause to reflect: Is it possible that the missioner treats my brother and sister Muslims as his own brothers and sisters without any intention of converting them? What new teaching is this?

In this part of the world, the need for tolerance and respect between religions is huge. Religiously inspired riots flared frequently in Gandhi's time; there is still fear of riots today. Gandhi believed that proselytization brought with it conflict. "The transference of allegiance from one fold to another and the mutual decrying of rival faiths gives rise to mutual hatred."

A question that Muslim men have put to me as a test is: "What will I receive if I become a Christian?" The majority of the inquirers are merely displaying their contempt for the alleged willingness of some missioners to tempt the poor and purchase their conversion. Although the missioners who strive to make converts this way are not principally Catholics, we Catholic missioners share their notorious reputation by association. Muslims' profoundly negative perception of all missioners will endure for as long as some missioners continue to stress the conversion of Muslims as the goal of mission in Bangladesh.

Twenty years of living closely with Muslims has taught me that they are quite suspicious of missioners, assuming that they do good to the poor solely in order to make converts to Christianity. Sad to say, there is some historical basis, in fact, for that perception. The most effective remedy for this jaundiced Muslim view is, in my experience, for the missioner to forswear conversion as the purpose of mission.

There are persons who tell me in private that they are willing to become Christians if I will reciprocate with a loan, a scholarship, or a job. They would use their conversion as a commodity to be bartered for material benefits provided by me. What does the Church tell me about dealing with such persons? The teaching is clear: "Material inducements carry a hint of coercion or a kind of persuasion that would be dishonorable or unworthy, especially when dealing with poor or uneducated people" (*Declaration on Religious Freedom*, Second Vatican Council). Where missioners are perceived to be sources of foreign largesse, as they are in Bangladesh, the temptation for some persons to convert in order to gain material advantages is great.

Making converts from among other Christian denominations also needs to be excluded. In a village twenty miles away from me, a community of Christians had lived united for half a century. A missioner from another denomination arrived and, finding himself unable to make converts from among the Muslims and Hindus in that locality, he turned his energies to the old Christians. That village is now divided between the two denominations. Their Muslim and Hindu neighbors ridicule the converters for having offered material inducements, and they poke fun at the converts who gave up their religion for a bribe. Peace is less in evidence now than before that preacher of the faith arrived. Christianity is derided in that locality.

It is not my purpose to preach the Christian faith by word of mouth to Muslims and Hindus. I try, rather, to convey that faith through my behavior and works of compassion. Whenever they see my attention and kindness bestowed on persons who are strangers to me, they ask me: "What gain is in it for you?" I reply: "Following Jesus' example gives my heart happiness. God's blessing is all the reward I want. My mother and father, sister and brothers, are overjoyed that their son and brother spends his life in this way because their generosity will also be eternally rewarded by God." Muslims and Hindus are responding to the inspiration provided by God through their own religious faith. I respond to the inspiration given by God through Christian faith. We all intend and are striving to do the will of God, Allah, Bhagavan. They do the will of God in their way; I do it in my way. Oftentimes, our responses are alike. I do not judge their religions to be lacking. After all, they are frequently moved by their faiths to do those acts of virtue and good works which my religion urges me to do.

Gandhi counseled: "If you want us to feel the aroma of Christianity, you must copy the rose. The rose irresistibly draws people to itself, and the scent remains with them." At the outset of my stay in Bangladesh, I paid a visit to an elderly missioner who had long years of experience working among Muslims. His story helped me to decide on the service I would offer to Muslims. This wise man had sought to convince and convert Muslims to Christianity during ten prime years of missionary endeavor. For, he explained, at that time, conversion was the focus of mission work. Try as he might, he was unable to convert a single Muslim to Christianity. Then one day, as he stood conversing with an educated young Muslim, they both observed a man sprawled in the gutter of the street. Two women wearing identical white garb appeared, approached the man, went down to him and ministered to him. When next the missionary looked at this Muslim acquaintance's face, he was surprised to find him in tears. The sisters' active compassion had touched him. The young Muslim did not thereafter seek to become a Christian. Islam also stresses mercy and compassion toward the afflicted. However, he did understand compassion better, thanks to the example of two Catholic sisters. Their practical illustration of love, no doubt, remains with him until this day. Good example irresistibly draws all persons of good will, no matter what their religion is, and makes them more aware of the possibilities to do and to be good. Although this example occurred years after Gandhi's death, he would have understood perfectly the tearful appreciation of the Bengali Muslim. "Do not preach the God of history, but show Him as He lives today through you"—this was Gandhi's advice to missioners. The two sisters had uttered not a word about religion to the man in the gutter. Yet they changed not only his life but also the lives of all who saw their love.

Bangladeshi Christians sometimes ask me: "What results do you have to show for years of living among Muslims?" I reply: "Nothing tangible," because there is no physical memorial to this work—no schools started, no parishes established, no cooperatives begun. However, I do seem to have a lot of Muslim friends and well-wishers, most of whom were initially suspicious of "the missionary." Later, they came to be surprised by his love for the poor and respect for their faith. These Muslims have ended up speaking respectfully, and sometimes even enthusiastically, about the missioner's life and the service he gives without expectation of reward. Trust and friendship are growing.

I have seen that Islam and Hinduism help these good people, give them guidance and comfort, and move them to practice virtue. This is not the place or time for Christians to press ahead with missionary themes from the past, e.g., Christianity is best, other religions and their rites are false or silly, conversion to Christianity is the only path to salvation. The Church encourages in Christians a new attitude toward other faiths, an attitude with which Gandhi would have been more comfortable and for which he is at least indirectly responsible.

I have read the Qur'an and the Hadith (the sayings and doings of the Prophet) of the Islamic faith and they have informed me. Even more enriching and broadening, however, have been personal contacts with Muslims and Hindus. In particular, conversations and friendship with Haji Abdul Mannan during my first year in Bangladesh added depth and warmth to my conviction that we are meant by God to be brothers and sisters to men and women of other faiths. More than anything else, close-range involvement with ordinary Muslims and Hindus has helped me to appreciate and respect other persons and their religions. I know that I have been enriched by close contact with them. They have enabled me to understand that persons holding to immensely diverse religions can share deeply many identical values. Through contact, I perceive that faith in God, under the banner of whatever religion, results in lives that are praiseworthy. Moreover, few things in life could lead me more surely to God than the certain knowledge that persons who believe in teachings dissimilar to Christian teachings also love God and practice virtue.

When I see Muslims giving alms, enduring the fast, offering prayers faithfully, or behaving mercifully or generously, it has the same kind of effect on me as the study of the solar system. That is, it expands my mind and heart. It gives evidence to me that there is more to other faiths than meets the eye. Like the universe, which is boundless and still expanding, so too is my admiration and appreciation for persons of every faith and for their faiths.

There is one God and there are many paths to God. All of the paths that lead to God are good. It is impossible to judge another's path because we are not on it. We see others' paths in a distorted way, from afar, from outside their souls wherein faith abides. Yet, we do see that many persons on other paths live virtuously. My experience is that hospitality, mercy, generosity, and tolerance characterize the Muslims I know.

When I see goodness in the lives of others, I affirm them in my heart. It seems fitting to me that a missioner, that is, a person whom Muslims regard as an official representative of the Christian faith, openly praises persons who act mercifully, pray, give alms, fast, and undertake the pilgrimage. How thought provoking it is for Muslims and Hindus when I praise their works. Their amazed reaction is: Can it truly be that a Christian missioner admires Muslims and Hindus?

Principal Matiur Rahman once told me: "Our religions have the potential to unite humankind. In fact, we use religion to keep ourselves apart." The inclination we have to always compare ourselves with others, combined with our ignorance of the inner lives of Muslims and Hindus, contributes to our false sense of superiority. We tend to be judgmental and to search for the things that separate us from other religions.

I thank God for Mahatma Gandhi. Gandhi demonstrated a life of dedication, concern for others, and daring in the cause of God, while professing a faith other than Christianity. He knew Christian teaching and regarded much of it as beautiful and true. He was close to numerous Christian missionaries and was invited by them to become a Christian. He refused these invitations because his own religion, Hinduism, satisfied his soul. He refused, also, because he saw little in the lives of Christians that could motivate him to request baptism. Gandhi was a seeker after truth, a man who was grateful to God for the compelling message of the Sermon on the Mount. One of his great services to Christians was to suggest that we do mission wrongly, or more, that we even go about mission in an unchristian manner. Because his knowledge and appreciation of Christianity was deep, his criticism of Christian mission methods deserves my attention. He claimed to know a mission approach which, if followed, would both benefit the people and advance the saving mission of Jesus. "A life of service and of uttermost simplicity is the best preaching." My experience during twenty years of living among his people is that Gandhi knew what he was talking about.

By the fruits of his life and his love for Jesus, we know Gandhi to have been a follower of Jesus, although not exclusively of Jesus. Because of Gandhi, I know that a Christ-like spirit can exist in unbaptized persons. His life and example prepare me to expect that heroic evangelical virtue can be exercised by those who are not formally Christians. Because I expect to find abundant goodness and virtue among Muslims and Hindus, I do find it. If I did not expect to find virtue among them, I would probably miss it.

I look at the Mahatma and think: How beautiful it is to be broadminded. To complain about the existence of other religions, or to view them as a threat to our Christian preeminence, reveals narrowness of vision—as if God cannot dwell within people who, though aware of the teachings of Christianity, choose to be or to remain Muslim or Hindu. How alike were the spirits of Gandhi and Pope John XXIII, who counseled in his last testament: "Love one another. Seek rather what unites, not what may separate you from one another."

God is greater than our hearts (1 John 3:20).

Life among the Faithful

--- ❖ ---

Last evening at 8:52, just minutes after I'd laid my tired body to rest beneath a mosquito net, a five- to ten-second earthquake rattled Bangladesh. Before three seconds of the quaking had passed, people on all sides of my hut were imploring Allah's mercy in tones born of terror in the face of an object of genuine fear. The implorings continued well beyond the quake.

Anyone who wants to hear a spontaneous outpouring of heartfelt prayer should be present in a Bengali Muslim neighborhood whenever an earthquake occurs or a furious gust of wind suddenly arises. Sometimes one hears the storm identified: "Cyclone!" But, more often than not, identification is of no concern. After all, Allah well knows what kind of storm his creatures are caught in. At that moment every word from every mouth is directed toward The Almighty. And the word most used to implore The Creator of storm and earthquake, fire and flood, is "Allah! Allaaaahhh! Allaaaaahhhhh!"

In the name itself is the cry for help, safety, salvation. "Save us from this storm! Help us, Almighty One! Be with us, Merciful One!" Such sentiments need not be explicitly expressed. They are embraced by the most important word in the Muslim vocabulary, the word imbibed from childhood through parents' frequent use of it, the name above all others, in which there is strength for the weak, comfort for the afflicted, and courage for the frightened. No people I have ever seen turn more quickly, expectantly, and hopefully toward their God than do Muslims in their moment of desperation.

"Allah!" is the basic Muslim prayer, for which all other words are merely an elaboration.

Headmaster Matiur Rahman, the gentleman who originally invited me to come to live in this town, no longer lives here himself. I sought him out to check on his gout. He said that he had gone to the rooftop the previous day and had observed on the street below a raggedly dressed woman entering a garbage bin in order to eat scraps of tomatoes that had been tossed aside. "Unfortunately," he noted, "I did not go down to her and tell her: 'Do not eat in this filth, but rather, come and eat whole tomatoes in my house.'" Then the headmaster launched into a long story about a king who had helped a man who had been assigned to assassinate him. The story, by Tolstoy, had deeply touched him. He concluded: "There are only three important questions in life, according to Tolstoy: When is the most important time? Who is the most important person? And what is the most important duty? The answers are: Now. The person in front of me. And to do good to that person."

The headmaster is a well-educated man. He has read broadly and is not only familiar with Western writers but knows chapter and verse of the Qur'an and Hadith of the Prophet of Islam. He could have cited any number of texts to make his point that we are our brothers' and sisters' keepers. But he chose to quote a Western Christian writer because Tolstoy's viewpoint so adequately reflects the headmaster's belief. He is confident that anything an eminent Christian may say about our attitude toward the poor will also explain how Muslims think of the poor. "Those who serve the poor serve Allah," summarizes that belief. Beyond that, however, the headmaster does not look to Christianity for views and answers. Christianity, in his mind, has forfeited its right to act as teacher by its hopelessly contradictory and stubbornly repeated blasphemy that God

A young man lifts his eyes and hands to Allah. Around his neck is the *tasbih* (Islamic rosary), upon which are recited the 99 beautiful names of God.

had a Son, and that Jesus, Son though he was, was defeated on the cross. The headmaster is satisfied that Jesus was a prophet, and he loves Jesus as a prophet. He also believes that Jesus himself pointed to the coming of Mohammed the Prophet when Jesus spoke of sending the Spirit. He feels that Christian belief is unreasonable and obstinate. He is not tempted or inclined in the least to investigate Christianity because of the glaring errors he perceives in the doctrines of sonship and suffering in God. He is secure in Islam. It makes good sense to him; it teaches him his relationship to Allah as well as the exercises he must do and the intention he must have in order to please The Creator. He feels superior to me, the Christian missionary, but is not for that reason unwilling to share with me a humbling example of his weakness. For Allah is merciful, and Allah's servants must be tolerant of others' weaknesses.

A twelve-year-old burn patient named Manik is lying in bed at the local hospital with his arms extended straight up to relieve the pain. Although he has been hospitalized for a week, he only started on antibiotics today when I came around to see him. His mother is so grateful; even though she does not use the word for thanks I can feel her gratitude. She is no older than thirty but looks older. The telltale bloatedness of malnutrition gives her cheeks a two-toned effect. Countless women of her age wear the same mask, the result of having skipped meals so that their sons and daughters could eat more. The brown *sharee* she wears is sewn together in many places with large white stitches; there is no need to tell anyone that she has no change of clothing. When I brought the prescribed medicine to her son, the mother's anxious face cracked into a glorious smile of relief. "You are my godfather," she said, taking my hand momentarily in hers. She may or may not know that I am a Christian. It would make no difference to her, under the circumstances. Her son is in need. I have proven my concern for her son. She has bestowed upon me her richest reward: the recognition that I have freely done what a "have" should do for a "have not," and so fostered a relationship that includes her son, herself, Allah, and me.

Often after I have done some kindness for a Muslim Bengali I have been similarly rewarded. Just as commonly, they express their gratitude by saying "After Allah comes you" in helping us through this difficulty. There is no exaggeration in that statement. What it means is that Allah is the solver and the alleviator of all problems; He is incomparable; none can share His importance. *All* praise belongs to Allah. After Him, but separated by a million billion trillion gradations, comes me. In this situation I am being used by the Almighty more than other human agents are. My part in overcoming this particular problem is great compared to that of other persons, but infinitesimally minuscule—nearly nothing—when compared to Allah's part. (The expression should be, "Awaaaayyyy after Allah comes you.")

I wonder if the centrality of Allah in the thinking of Muslim Bengalis can help to explain why one seldom hears a simple "Thank you" in Bangladesh. To single out a fellow human being in order to give him or her thanks without explicitly and emphatically recognizing that Allah is the actual source of the benefit received would be unacceptable—so conscious is the grateful Muslim that every single benefit in life comes to us from The Best Giver (one of the 99 descriptive names of Allah).

After several hours in a small sailboat I arrived in Nikhli. Here I would be able to see how the people in outlying areas were coping with the flood. People had evacuated their farms and homes and come to the higher ground near the bazaar. Hundreds had found shelter in a primary school. Men, women and children gathered around me, standing ankle deep in mud, to learn what their unexpected visitor had to say. They had time on their hands. Moreover, the circumstances that the flood had placed them in had made them especially sober and reflective.

"What caused the flood?" I asked.

"Flood waters came down from India" answered a man, and no one expanded on his reply. Apparently none of them understands that deforestation in the Himalayas is a precise cause.

"Who did this?" I asked.

"Allah-tallah," replied another man with respect and wonder in his tone.

"Why did He do it?" I asked.

"Who knows the mind of Allah?!" one replied. "To punish us for our sins. What else?" he added.

"Which sins?" I asked.

"For our failure to pray and to fast, mainly," responded one. He continued: "Also for cheating, stealing, robbing, and the coercing that some do. We are all paying for that."

Another man confirmed him, saying: "In a word, for our singing songs while we should have been praying and fasting."

A heavy mist had just been pierced by the rising sun at 8:30 A.M. I had been bicycling in the same direction for more than an hour on the feast day of the Three Kings (Epiphany) before it occurred to me that I was headed straight east. One year ago, on this same route, I had treated a naked madman to a meal in the village of Korgaon. Today I stopped to eat at the same hotel and could hardly believe it when I found that very man, Ashraf Ali, sitting at a table beside the door. He is much better now, and wears clothes. Ashraf remembered me and the meal of bread with vegetables he had taken. We enjoyed a friendly conversation today and shook hands in parting. Then he put both his open hands over his heart, to carry my blessing there. "By your mercy I am better," he claimed. A year ago I told him that I would continue to bless him, and he believes it has been effective.

When I reached home late in the afternoon, little old Mofis came to my door. He was smiling but ill. His feet are still puffed up with edema as they have been for weeks. "Is your health any better?" I inquired. "Yes, by the grace of Allah, the swelling has decreased," he replied. I offered him a few more of the inexpensive pills. "I ask Allah to bless you," he said in thanks, with feeling. "And I call on Allah to bless you, Mofis," I told the good man. When two persons having divergent faiths accept and appreciate the blessings of one another, is that not the best sort of dialogue?

A priest asked me for my thoughts on the evangelization of Christian religious personnel by the poor. It seems to me that the poor evangelize us by giving us various types of good example. They instruct us in patience by their patience under adversity. They edify us by their uncomplaining struggles. They inspire us by undergoing suffering without becoming bitter. They encourage us to face our own problems more bravely by grappling with the pain in their lives. They teach us about the simplicity with which one can live a human life. They offer us a model for prayer life by their dependence on God: that is, in times of great need they look to God before all else. They do not appeal to God secondly or lastly after other possibilities have failed them. When we witness their efforts to survive with dignity amidst the hardships they constantly encounter, they help us to put into perspective our own overblown problems. Through the struggling poor we begin to understand how good God is to us and how stingy we are with our thanksgiving to God. If we think about them deeply enough, they put us to shame. For, though they are oppressed, they can still laugh and sing. Still, the safest answer to give to the question "How do the poor evangelize us?" is to recall that God is with them. God is a mystery to us, and God's way of working through the poor is beyond our analysis.

When I accompanied Aladi to the hospital, the doctor diagnosed cancer and admitted her for a week of treatment. Afterward she returned to her village. Every Saturday during the remaining months of her life I stopped at her hut, held her hand, and spoke of Allah's love for her. On one occasion, after I had told her "Aladi, remember, Allah loves you" she looked me in the eye, smiled through her pain, and in a firm, clear voice improved upon my statement. "*You* love me!" she declared.

How correct she was. What she acknowledged is, I believe, precisely what Christian mission among Bangladeshi Muslims must illustrate: unconditional love. We love Muslims as they are and not in view of their becoming Christians. We view them as already good and worthy of our respect, our trust, and our fraternal affection.

I had been told that somewhere in the town lives a Christian nurse who is married to a Muslim. Finally, today I met her. Jasinta is from Toomilia, the center of the largest congregation of Catholic religious sisters in all Bangladesh. Jasinta met her future husband while she was studying nursing in Mymensingh. They married and now she has two sons and a secure position as a staff nurse in the district town of her husband, Ali. She is a Muslim in the sense that she accepted Islam before marrying Ali. She is a Christian in the sense that the formation she received as a girl and follows as an adult is based on the teaching of the Church; she never renounced Jesus Christ.

I asked her if she was free to visit her home village. She said it is possible to go there for one week each year. "Can you attend Mass when you go home?" I asked. "No," she said, "because some of the local people would be offended by it." Since she accepted Islam, they feel that she has left the Christian community for the Muslim community and that, if she were to attend Mass, she should be made to feel the traitor. Once upon a time, Jasinta told me, she had dreamed of taking vows as a religious. Now, during a yearly one-week vacation, she cannot even practice openly the faith of her upbringing. What is she to do? I urged Jasinta to perform her Muslim duties with all the love in her Christian heart.

As long as Jasinta is in this predicament she must make the best of it. Her husband and his entire extended family, to which she has joined herself, are Muslims. I have not heard of a Muslim or Christian family so lenient that they encourage the spouse of their son to remain in the religion of her youth—unless it is the same as his. Jasinta could and would disrupt Ali's entire family if she were to insist on practicing the Christian faith openly. Only an extraordinarily strong person could endure the tension and ill will that it would create against her. Besides, it would probably cause Ali to divorce her. So, why not urge her to call on the Lord in the secrecy of her heart? God Who sees all things in secret will surely not forsake her. God knows Jasinta did not embrace Islam because of disgust for Jesus and His teachings. She converted to Islam solely for the sake of the marriage. If Ali were to agree to become a Christian, and all his family blessed the move, then they could be at Mass together next Sunday. However, he is comfortable in Islam. Although Jasinta is uncomfortable in Islam, she can bear it as a cross. She cannot openly profess that she is a follower of the Lord Jesus. But no one can force the affections of her heart as she prays to God behind closed doors.

Where can we look to find the Lord Jesus? According to the startling revelation recorded by St. Matthew, we do not have to search far: "As often as you did good to these lowly ones, you did it to me." Jesus identifies Himself with those who suffer. Whenever we seek, find, and assist a sufferer we do it to Jesus. Therefore, one place we are sure to find Jesus is wherever human beings suffer.

A Baptist missionary once proclaimed to me that all Muslims must be baptized into Christianity in order to be saved. "Those who do not become Christians are damned to eternal hell." That categorical perception spurs him on to conquer others for Christ. Still, I wonder: Was Jesus joking when He taught us to discover Him in sufferers? Most of the suffering persons I know and meet each day are Muslims. Jesus, it seems to me, identified Himself with them purely on the basis of their suffering. Not because they are Christian or Jewish or Muslim or Hindu sufferers, but simply because they suffer. Surely those persons with whom Jesus identifies Himself are not candidates for hell. According to Jesus, identification with Him does not depend on one's religion or lack of a religion.

The reputation of Bangladesh as a disaster area might make one think that when I speak of suffering I mean the physical kind only: hunger, disease, destruction, and bodily deprivations. However, I know from my own middle-class background that suffering can be present even in the healthiest body. My first year of college was a time of misery for me. I was greatly bothered that I had no purpose in life. I was studying successfully but did not know for what end. It made me feel miserable that I could not envision what I would do with my life. Never before that eighteenth year of life, nor since then, have I experienced a comparable misery. My misery was spiritual, lasted for one year, and nearly overwhelmed me. Therefore, I would never say that the really significant suffering in the world occurs solely in the Third World. Everybody's suffering is significant. The suffering Jesus is nowhere absent. We have only to encourage one another.

The vast majority of Bangladeshi Muslims are tolerant of other people's religions. It is easy to look on their tolerance as a sign of their salvation. In the four towns where I have spent the better part of two decades, people accept me. Jesus spoke about these people: "He who accepts anyone I send accepts me, and in accepting me accepts him who sent me" (John 13:20).

There are exceptions, of course. But the exceptional ones do not outweigh the tolerance that the majority of Muslims bear toward persons of proven good will. Yesterday a man told me: "If you ever leave this place, our stomachs will churn for you!" Bengalis use that expression to emphasize how much they will miss someone. So, there are Muslims who more than accept the Christian missioner; they like him.

In the bazaar recently a *maulavi* [graduate in theology] was sitting in his vegetable stall as I shopped for supper. "You must become a Muslim. You must become a Muslim," he repeated at least a dozen times. I was tempted to reply sarcastically, but checked myself. He was cheerful and uttered the words as if in invitation, pleasantly. In fact, he was complimenting me. He wants me on the side of Islam. Not only does he accept and like me. He wishes for my salvation and for my perfection as a man. It troubles him that I do not share, explicitly, his religious faith. The appropriate path for anyone who spends his or her life helping others is to do all things under the banner of Islam, he thinks. He knows Islam is true; he wishes I knew it, too.

Four boys ran up and shook my hand as I walked to a neighborhood store. Minutes later, on the return, they shook my hand again. Young men on the street, shop keepers and tea stall operators customarily shout out "Bob Brother!" whenever they notice me passing by on a bicycle. Older men who know me often salute. No doubt there are some Muslims and Hindus living in this district who hate me, but they have not gone public with it yet. The closest I can recall having come during this past year to feeling someone's hatred for me was when a missionary priest (of European origin) shrilly confronted me. In a voice filled with contempt and emotion he accused me of having left the Catholic faith because, in my dealings with Muslims, I do not dwell on the redeeming death of the Son of God. He's right; I don't. He's wrong; I'm quite Catholic.

The kingdom of God is a "time" of earthly concord. Persons of all races and religions will live harmoniously in that kingdom. I announce it each day while speaking to Muslims about the Catholic Christian attitude toward them, and toward Hindus. "We are one family," I explain. "We are brothers and sisters all. You were born Muslim and that is good. Be good Muslims. I was born Christian and am trying to be a follower of Jesus. I do not desire that you become Christians. I desire that you become good and happy Muslims. We have to respect one another and work together to help humankind. That way is Allah's way: open to other people, accepting of them, and hoping for them."

I do not recall ever having been contradicted while speaking in this manner. Most of the time my partners in conversation tell me that they believe what I am saying. People see so much of factionalism and selfishness every day that they are ready to listen to a prophet of harmony.

"Whoever does the will of my Father in heaven is my brother, my sister, and my mother" (Matthew 12:50). So Jesus tells us. According to Him, the one who performs God's will is close to Himself. It is hard not to look upon the majority of Muslims and Hindus here as fitting into that definition of spiritual relationship. The majority of the people I see are obviously struggling to do the right things with scrawny resources. The unmistakably clear will of Allah for most of these adults is that they faithfully provide food, shelter, clothing and other emergency necessities to the families entrusted to them by Allah. It seems to me that they pursue that goal with a determination and constancy that would be inexplicable were it not for grace.

One of the most edifying works for which I admire Muslims is the practice of regular prayer. I can always find Muslims who, individually or in a group, stop their other occupations in order to offer

A girl learns to read the Quran in Arabic.

prayer at five set times between dawn and evening. Not all Muslims do so; not even a majority of the adults do so, consistently. But the ones who do pray regularly maintain among all the Muslims of their neighborhoods and villages a consciousness of the importance of prayer. It seems to me that among the five pillars of Islam (i.e., the confession of faith, prayer, almsgiving, fasting, and pilgrimage to Mecca) prayer is the one which best illustrates what Muslims think of Allah and of themselves in relation to Allah. Allah is the transcendent Creator, and they are Allah's adoring creatures.

Fatima, a beautiful young mother who lives across the way with her husband Abul and two children, is still weak from having given birth to a son three months ago. Her head spins, she is lethargic and has poor circulation. And now she is fasting. I suggested to her that, in her weakened condition, fasting may not be good for her or the baby. The suggestion only made her smile. She knows what is expected of adult Muslims.

Monju was all enthusiasm for the annual fast when we happened to meet at the tubewell at 3:30 A.M. on the second day of fasting. "Fasting is good for one's health!" he declared. For him that is true. He needs to lose some weight. But for 90 percent of the Muslims in Bangladesh I am less convinced of the benefits of fasting. Take, for example, my neighbors on the east side. They did not stir from their mats despite the amplified calls from the tower of the mosque which urged all to "Rise and eat!" before the 4:44 A.M. deadline. They are sickly and weak, and aware that they cannot withstand this discipline. They need to take food during the day, and will do so quietly. Any medical doctor would say that they have made a wise decision. But some *maulavis* would reprimand them for laxity.

In the evening, two *maulavis* paid me a visit. The younger one, Badruzzaman, is a local man with whom I had conversed before.

This time he was accompanied by an older follower of the Prophet, one who is more learned and experienced in matters Islamic, named Abdul Bari. Bari is from the capital city and has come to this district town for a few days, on a teaching mission at our neighborhood mosque. Earlier in the day, he told me, he had seen me conversing with a sickly woman. As he stood to leave my hut, Bari pledged to pray that I would embrace Islam. I smiled ruefully and assured him that I am a Christian forever. Bari was quick to explain: "By praying for your conversion I mean no offense to you. In fact, I believe your life of service is beautiful. I merely want to see Muslims accept your example. Muslims will not follow your example as long as you remain a Christian. But if you were to become a Muslim, hundreds would follow in your footsteps. They would embrace your feet and enter upon your path of service to the needy. Think about it!" he solemnly challenged me as the two pious men departed in order to perform their evening prayer at the mosque.

Bari's insistence on having exclusively Muslim role models for the Muslim faithful reminds me of another *maulavi* who once came to see me. Bayejid lived near me and had observed me closely for more than a year. He wanted me to know how happy it made him to see a Christian serving Muslims. He also wished to be known as one who serves. "But what can I do?" he asked me. "I am a poor man, my teaching keeps me busy, and I have a family." We tried to think of ways in which he could serve and then I offered him a concrete suggestion. He could visit the hospital wards, and if he found illiterate patients there who wished to send news to their village homes, Bayejid could offer to write their letters and post them. A smile came across my friend's face. He thought it was a splendid idea and departed my house in good spirits. The following day, however, Bayejid returned to see me. Dejectedly, he admitted that he could not carry out his plan of the evening before. Why? I inquired. "If I do that sort of a thing," Bayejid explained, "people will say that I have become a Christian."

Why isn't it possible for a Muslim to follow the inspiring ex-

ample of a Christian, and vice versa? Surely it should be possible.
People of all faiths lead graced lives.

Someone informed me that a Christian nurse had been assigned
to the small, remote hospital that is run by the Red Crescent Society
in the village of Telighati, twelve miles from town. Two weeks later,
at my first opportunity, I went to look her up. Monjoli was pleased
to have a Christian visitor. She reminded me that I had known her
ten years earlier while she was in training at Mirzapur Hospital.
Monjoli is not the only new staff member at the Red Crescent Hospital. Doctor Mohammed Ali has also recently arrived there to serve
as medical officer. He is a single man; his mother cooks for him.
During our conversation he made a request. "Please give me a cross
[i.e., a crucifix] to wear around my neck." Why do you want it? I
inquired. "Because I believe in Jesus Christ. Although I am a Muslim, I believe in Jesus."

The doctor's request surprised me—not because of his love for
Jesus, for I have never heard a Muslim say a word against Jesus. That
would be as unthinkable to a Muslim as speaking ill about the Prophet
Mohammed; it would be blasphemy. The young Muslim's desire to
wear a crucifix was what amazed me. Christians think of the crucifixes they wear as signs of identification. The crucifix says: I am a
Christian. Apparently, the primary meaning of the crucifix will be
otherwise for the doctor; it will be a sign of his personal devotion to
the Prophet Jesus.

The Muslim equivalent of the Christian crucifix is, in Bangladesh,
the *tabiz*. This tiny, book-shaped metal container encloses a piece of
paper upon which is written a verse or a chapter from the Qur'an,
or one of Allah's 99 names. The container is usually attached to a
man's or woman's bicep by a shoelace, or else tied to one's waist by
a string. Muslims who wear the *tabiz* experience feelings similar to
those of Catholic Christians who wear medals and crucifixes. The
names and the words of Allah are powerful to protect, to console,
and to remind the wearer.

Mostafa the rickshaw puller is spending idle days in the eye hospital where he is accompanying his recently blinded son, Manik. By the time Manik's hospitalization ends, his father will have spent almost a month there. This is the longest vacation Mostafa has taken in his arduous life. Mostafa was with me when I handed over money to the eye surgeon as payment for a silicon band to encircle Manik's detached retina. When the doctor left the room, Mostafa and I stood alone. Tears came to his eyes. I spoke for a while, but he did not reply. He was overcome by emotion that a non-family member had given for his son more money than he could earn in a month of exhausting labor.

It is usually the women who give voice to the feelings of the poor toward a foreigner who strives to be useful to them.

Recently I encountered two women walking to a village. "Abba, where are you going?" asked one, using the same word for father that Jesus used when speaking to The Father: Abba. I had assisted the woman in some small way, months earlier, and because of that she still felt close to me. Most often it is from women that I hear the word *Abba*. Men may use it too, but as it is a term of affection they use it less often–and not at all within earshot of me. It is noteworthy that the Bengali Islamic culture retains a term that endears Jesus to us all: Abba/Daddy.

Many of the women, after receiving from me the advice they need to overcome illness, or the medicine they require in order to improve, have bestowed on me a name above other earthly names. "You are my father because you do a father's work!" they proclaim.

Week number one of the yearly great fast is under way. As I bicycled this morning to the village of Tenga, an elderly farmer hailed me. He spoke of his gastrointestinal complaint. In order to get relief within a few days he would have to take some tablets three times a day. "But I am fasting," he replied good naturedly. I said that the choice was up to him: Maintain the fast and remain sickly, or barely break the fast (by swallowing the noonday pill) and improve. "I have not transgressed the fast, even once, since I was a ten-year-old boy," he stated with pride. And that is how he informed me of his choice. He would rather suffer the added inconvenience from gastric pain than the humiliation that would come from being unable to keep the fast.

Bengali Muslims really do want to keep the fast. A good number of them do not. Their jobs are too heavy to permit it, and they are too poor to take time off in order to fast. They cannot throw cargo or pull carts or pump rickshaws on empty stomachs. There are some others who have convinced themselves that fasting is a backward practice and not something they will allow custom or culture to force upon them. However, the vast majority genuinely do want to fast, for Allah, and to confirm that they are part of the community of Islam. I pray for their success.

I have been living in this town almost three years but only today did I meet a person who must be classified as one of its most unique inhabitants. Ekram Hossain Talukdar is a retired teacher and artist. His pride and joy in life is to have supported twenty-nine young persons in their educational careers, from grade one through college. At present, he is still in shock and grief from the accidental death, at age 17, of a favorite student of his: Babul. So attached to that obedient Hindu youth was the Muslim benefactor that Talukdar built a beautiful Hindu temple to commemorate Babul. Fellow Muslims have reproached him for it. "Why would a Muslim waste so much money on a Hindu shrine when there are so many other real needs to address?" they ask. "Why would a Muslim dedicate anything to a Hindu?" ask others. Talukdar replies that there is only one religion, of which Muslims, Hindus, Buddhists, Christians, and Jains are all a part. As for the diversity of religions in the world, he looks on them as proof of Allah's unfathomable plan. "Eyes are beautiful organs," he says, "but would a person be balanced if he were all eyes? Is the most beautiful flower garden composed solely of red roses?" he asks, pointing out the beauty that arises precisely from the diversity of flowers. "So it is with religions," he judges. "All of them taken together are beautiful and complementary. Taken singly, however, their loveliness is less." This Muslim teacher perceives that when people compare religions they become exclusivistic, envious of the beauty in others, and greedy for acclaim as "the best religion."

Motiur Rahman is an educator. He is also a religious person and it is about religion that he has been thinking most deeply during this past year. Simultaneously, his gout has grown worse and he has undergone a double hernia operation. The pain and inconvenience embolden him to speak out on truths he holds. "All persons are equal; that is a fact. In the eyes of the Almighty we are no more and no less than all the others. Humankind should be one—a community of equals. But we are divided. What divides us? Religion is the most divisive facet of human life. We cling to our religions and imagine that others should not cling to theirs. Everyone thinks that his or her religion is the best one, and that the other fellow is in error." Religion is so often used, misused, and manipulated to drive people apart that Rahman quotes favorably the saying that "Religion is the refuge of scoundrels." Rahman is an interesting man because, as far as appearances go, he is a solid, conservative Muslim. One would never find him without his prayer cap on his head. His image is Islamic and his manner is pious. Yet, the things he has to say about religion are a challenge to fellow Muslims. He is a man who holds that the most intolerable aspect of life is the intolerance generated by one religion against another.

A lovely girl named Aleema, aged seven, came to my door as I was putting up wet clothing to dry. "Bob Brother, I saw you in my dream," she announced. Taken aback, I inquired: "Was I on my bicycle when you saw me?" She replied sweetly: "No. You had come to our home and we were feeding you a good meal."

Now I understand that Muslims are not only hospitable, but that some of them even dream about offering hospitality. It is a dream I cannot remember ever having had. In fact, I do not recall ever having dreamed about eating anything. And so much the less have I ever dreamed about feeding others. If it is true, therefore, that we dream of the things in life that are really significant to us, then the dream of a small Muslim girl, a dream in which wonderful food is offered to a visitor, would seem to say that she, and they, have their priorities in divine order. To offer hospitality to strangers is a requirement of Islam, no less than of Christianity. But to dream about offering hospitality is proof that Allah's holy will has been internalized in one's heart.

In a few weeks' time Christians will celebrate Christmas. That, however, is of no consequence to Muslims. Rather, every morning there are signs to be seen of the Islamic revival which is occurring in this neighborhood. The *muezzin* [crier of the hours of prayer] calls from the mosque, using his microphone and the amplifier perched atop the minaret of the mosque. Lone messengers stride through residential areas. All of them are shouting out the same message about optimal behavior. "It is better to be in the mosque than in the home," they say, and "It is better to pray than to sleep." Winter is the time of this outreach. It is cool; the energy required for house-to-house campaigning is present. They convince and cajole one another to attend the mosque and to join in the *namaz* [community prayer] there. Some evenings there are up to three separate meetings in the mosque, and the pious ones are treated to talks on Islam given by imported preachers. During other weeks the men participate in apostolic teaching missions, called *tablig*, to other villages in order to enliven the Islamic faith. Summertime would be too hot for such enthusiasm.

Surrounded by his family, Mohammed, the young man in the
chair, sits for a final photograph. Perhaps it is his first photo, too,
but we know it is his last. He broke his spine falling from a tree.
When doctors told him there was nothing to be done he ceased
to eat, thus speeding his demise and saving his family the
hardship of feeding an extra, nonproductive member.

On the rugged road that led back to the town a rickshaw puller stood beside his loaded rickshaw van on the south side of a small bridge. The bridge was too high for him to ascend by his own efforts. He was hoping that an acquaintance would pass by and that the two of them could push the laden van uphill and then ease it down the hill on the other side. No acquaintance came. Finally I happened along and stopped. "May I help you?" I inquired. "Oh, no!" he replied. "You are a *murobbi manus* [respectable person]." Respectable persons, it seems, are not expected to soil their hands or bend their backs to do labor of this sort. Dismounting, I set my bicycle aside. Beside him I leaned my weight on the van, pressing my shoulder and forehead against sacks filled with raw rice. When we had scaled the height we rested before slowly descending the other side of the bridge. As I picked up my bike to continue the journey, he turned to look my way. Neither of us said anything. Having done something constructive together, we are now close. Probably more is done to create trust, respect, and affection between people of various religions and diverse economic status by our pitching in to accomplish tasks together than would be created through any number of sermons, lectures, and seminars.

A husky, white-bearded, energetic *maulavi* with whom I had met just once previously sat down beside me in the small boat that would carry us across the Brahmaputra River. Pulling a small vial of perfume out of his pocket he offered to douse me on the wrist. No thanks, I demurred. But others in the boat were glad to accept. He pressed the mouth of the tiny bottle against the wrists of all who extended their arms toward him. Then, he chided me. "Why do you refuse? Jesus used perfume!" he protested. I did not recall any scriptural passage, whether Islamic or Christian, which claimed that. I replied: "It is not important for me." "But," the teacher reasoned, "you must follow Jesus' example, for He is your Prophet." "Ah, yes," I responded, "but it is only necessary for a Christian to imitate Jesus in matters which are essential. Love of neighbor is the most essential." The teacher of Islam listened in silence. Fellow passengers, all Muslims, waited for him to parry my remark. He did not. He was waiting, rather, for me to explain further the Christian view of following God's Prophet. I continued: "If anyone says 'I love Allah' but refuses to assist someone in greater need than himself, he lies. He is a hypocrite. Can a person love the unseen Creator if he refuses to love his neighbor, if he refuses to help Allah's creature who is in need?" After a short pause, the *maulavi* answered thoughtfully: "We think alike. Your religion and mine are the same."

By and large, Muslims do not like what they hear of Christianity's central doctrines—the Trinity or salvation through Jesus Christ. But in matters of morality and the need to live merciful lives, there could hardly be a people closer to Christians than are Muslims.

Eyes closed and meditating, I seemed to fellow passengers to be asleep as our train rumbled southward. Beside me, a heavy-set man asked the passengers who sat facing him about me: "Who is he?" Two young men answered him with as much information as they had. "He serves the poorest sick persons." "His brothers and sisters support him from the U.S.A. He does not work for a non-governmental organization (NGO)." "He eats vegetables." The inquirer remained silent afterwards, apparently satisfied with their answers. As was I. Although the two respondents had not defined me in the same terms I would have used, they did offer enlightenment. Besides, how many of us perceive ourselves as others do? What part of the young men's explanation will be remembered by the inquiring passenger? Perhaps the part about vegetables. The people of Bangladesh have a great memory for foodstuffs. If someone eats differently than they do, he or she is identified with odd eating habits. He or she becomes the subject of curious, wonder-filled conversations.

A jolly acquaintance whom I frequently see whenever I visit the orthopedic hospital seized my hand and shook it vigorously. "Whom have you brought to us today?" he inquired cheerfully. I nodded toward Shah Ali, a rickshaw puller whose hip had been ruined in an accident. Then, inspired by his appreciation for the good works of others which conscientious Bengali Muslims all seem to have, he began to address a military officer standing nearby. He boasted to him and to all within earshot about me. "We wear the *tupi* [prayer cap] and clean ourselves up in order to be fit for saying prayer." (Here, he modeled the position in which he and fellow Muslims pray, gazing heavenward and holding his upturned hands before his chest in a gesture of worship.) "But this man is practicing Islam. *Practicing it!*" Then he thrust his forefinger at me and continued to hold me under his good-natured severity, as if I were being accused of practicing virtue secretly. Then, he pronounced his judgment: "This man follows the example of the Prophet!" That got me. For the only prophet I claim to follow is Jesus, even though this Muslim brother was crediting me with something which, to his way of thinking, is even greater. He sees every work of mercy as a reflection of his Prophet.

Deep conversations sometimes occur when we least expect them. Two nurses were conversing at the local hospital when I ventured to ask one of them a question about a patient in her ward. Suddenly, at my approach, she launched a whole new topic of conversation. "There is no mediator between man and Allah," she preached mischievously at me. "Neither priests nor *maulavis* can be go-betweens for people.

Rather, each person stands before the Creator on his or her own merits."

As I am in essential agreement with what she said, I did not contradict the woman. Not only do I agree with her, I admire the vision of equality among all people which informs the practice of Islam. Any pious Muslim, for example, can lead Islamic prayer. His role, even then, is simply to guide the prayer of the assembly. He does not mediate between God and people. Muslims seem to believe that the essential feature of Christian priesthood is to serve as go-between, to mediate between heaven and earth. They imagine that the Christian priest attempts to do more than to preside. He sets himself up as an intermediary and, thereby, usurps God's power. If there are Christian priests who behave in that manner, and who encourage lay Christians to treat them accordingly, I regret it. For each person *is* responsible for his or her own salvation, and it is both Islamic and Christian to think so.

In the village of Hashil an elderly, sickly man was resting on a mat and staring straight ahead. He was scarcely aware of the fact that I was looking at his eyes, so severe had his condition become. Cataracts, I told myself. I said to him: "I think that your health is so poor that no doctor will agree to operate on your eyes." His reply was immediate and touched with disdain: "I want no operation. What need have I for eyesight? My sight belongs to Allah. I am not the owner of these eyes. If Allah wishes for me to see again, then I shall again see. If Allah wishes otherwise, then I am satisfied. Allah is my everything: my sight, my life, my future." His spontaneously offered *ferverino* had been so unrehearsed and convincing that I suspected I had met a saint. The frail old man exemplified indestructible faith that is enthroned in a ruined body. This compelling witness of faith in the Best Provider sees something more important than physical reality. He speaks and behaves as if Allah were quite near to him because it is so.

Professor Mojammel Haque tramped through the recently cut rice field on the eastern side of my house and greeted me jauntily at the door. He could hardly finish his greeting, so anxious was he to tell me what he feels when he sees an American living so modestly. "I tell you, Brother Bob, I am highly satisfied. You are living as the Prophet said: 'O Lord, let me live where the humble ones dwell, and then let me share their abode with you for eternity.'" What strikes me is not simply the professor's enthusiasm and approval, but rather his interpretation of the Hadith which he quoted to me. I had read the four large volumes of the Hadith, but it never occurred to me to apply them to myself. The professor, on the other hand, sees shades of his Prophet in my way of life. I try to live simply because Jesus did so. Professor sees an imitation of the Prophet Muhammed.

Jahanara's singing awoke me at 1:30 A.M. and was the reason for my oversleeping after I had succeeded in getting back to sleep. Her song, as is her custom, was long and religious. Whenever she sings, in fact, it is a prayer. She has much to pray about. Jahanara is almost blind and makes her living begging. She has much to be grateful for, also. Both her sons have been accepted into the local government orphanage. And, since last week, her new bamboo house is in place, complete with a tin roof. Begging and saving have rewarded her. Correction: Allah has rewarded her faithfulness, and it is to Allah that Jahanara gives all the credit.

❖

Near the end of my meditation period, at the dawn of a new day, Nizam's trembling voice reached my ears. He sat on a mat directly in front of his hut, and with eyes shut and hands upturned entreated Allah with tears. Every day he begins with this prayer, mix-

ing the content of orthodox Islamic prayer with the form of prayer
favored by Sufis. It always catches my attention to hear a grown
workman weeping at prayer. No doubt it also catches the attention
of the One to whom it is addressed.

In the darkness of the seventh day of fasting, Jahanara was praying, once again, for all to hear. She always prays distinctly, spontaneously, and with volume. During this night's conversation with
the Creator she said something I had heard her mention before. "By
my prayer I give witness to Allah," she proclaimed. Another neighbor, Jabeda, could not help hearing it also. She understood it as a
claim to self-righteousness, implying that those who pray less publicly than Jahanara fail to give witness to the primacy of Allah in
their lives. Jabeda retorted indignantly: "You are not the only one
who prays." What Jabeda could have answered is recorded in the
Christian scriptures (Matthew 6:6), for that is the way Jabeda prays—
out of sight and quietly.

Faith-filled, praying people surround me.

Early in the afternoon a man from this neighborhood came to
speak with me. He slipped inside my house and squatted beside the
place where I was sitting to write a weekly letter to Mom and Dad.
"I want to become a Christian," he said in a low tone. After a short
pause I asked him to come outside and point out his home to me.
He indicated a hut north of where we stood. I called upon the adults
in my compound to identify the man for me, and informed them:
"This man has asked to become a Christian." Then, to the man, I
stated something that is obvious to him—but that he feels certain
no missionary believes: "Muslims should be good Muslims. Christians should be good Christians. Are you a Muslim?" I inquired,
without really needing to. "Yes," he replied. "Islam is good," I continued, "and Hinduism and Christianity are good. Be a good follower of whatever is your religion." Nizam, then, appeared on the
scene, and drummed the message home. "We are all brothers, Mus-

lims and Christians, here. Do not come to this place seeking conversion." After the fellow had slipped quietly away, Nizam spoke disdainfully of the prospective convert's true purpose.

"I know that fellow. He is merely looking to receive something material from you, and nothing else." Nizam expressed well what has been my consistent experience with persons who have come to me for the avowed purpose of "becoming Christian." I think it is a good idea in Bangladesh to be rather curt with such opportunists so that the word will get around: Do not waste your time trying to hoodwink the missionary, or "tempt" him to enroll you in his religion. How, I wonder, can genuine respect between followers of different religions ever exist as long as one side is convinced that the other side has the conversion of Muslims as its sole objective?

Jahanara began to praise Allah at 1:00 A.M. and, as usual, I was awakened by it. So was Nizam. When he had heard enough he exploded, berating the young widow. "I have worked all day long and I want to rest! Give me some peace, woman!" From the other side of my hut Chan joined in, bitterly criticizing Jahanara. "There is a time for everything! Worship also has its time!" A heated, half-hour-long quarrel ensued. Over and over Jahanara returned to her single line of defense: "What I do within the confines of my own house I have the right to do!" Interestingly, no one disputed that principle. It amazed me that I had not heard this sort of battle before, for Jahanara has often broken into the praises of Allah during the still of the night. Nobody had complained. I was even beginning to imagine that other adults were sleeping through it—that is, that only I was being disturbed. Now I know differently. Yet, I have never seen people with a greater tolerance for invasive noise than Bengalis. Very rarely do I hear them crab about oppressive (and, in my case, intimidating) volume. (The ear doctor told me three months ago: "You've lost a bit of hearing in your left ear. Have you been subjected to loud noises?" I grinned at him and replied: "I live in

Early in the morning the mosque is used as a school to teach Arabic to the boys. (Girls come at an even earlier hour.) Every Muslim boy is expected to master some Arabic chapters from the Quran in order to recite them while praying.

Bangladesh, don't I?") Jahanara's behavior convinces me that home is not only a man's castle but also a privileged place within which a Muslim woman may express what she wants to express, and as she wishes, to her neighbors.

The children of this neighborhood are so anxious to see the end of the month of fasting (Ramzan) that they are trying to coax the moon to accommodate them. At 6:15 P.M., just a few minutes after the signal had sounded to end fasting for day number 29, approximately fifteen young children gathered near the water pump in order to search the heavens for signs of the new moon. Not finding anything, they pretended that they had. Pointing skywards and urging others to do the same, the children feigned a deliriously happy discovery. "Ramzan is over! Eid will be tomorrow!" Yusuf proclaimed as he hopped around the compound. But their claim is a fake. No one will be able to see the moon for at least another two hours. And then, if the moon is seen, the official moon-sighting committee—a group of religious professionals living in the capital—will verify it. That news will be broadcast over radio and television. Then, if the committee does, indeed, sight the moon, the kids will seem to be prescient. On the other hand, if the moon is not sighted, then the children's premature shouts of joy will count as practice for tomorrow evening's certain end of the fast. They will have learned a lesson, too: Allah cannot be coerced.

At 8:20 P.M. it was announced to a suspense-filled nation that the committee had sighted the Eid moon. The children of Bager Hat neighborhood are vindicated. The Almighty, it seems, can go along with a joke.

Alomgir the *maulavi* was making the rounds of our neighborhood to collect two *takas* (the equivalent of 5 U.S. cents) per family, and recording it in a large red ledger. Money is needed to continue building the local mosque. At the rate of two *takas* per family per month, "how much longer will you need to complete the project?" I asked. "A lifetime," Alomgir replied good-naturedly. Patience he has. One of the most inspiring examples for a Christian to behold in Bangladesh is the spirit with which Muslims undertake the building of a mosque. They know that it will require years to complete the project. Yet, they jump into the effort with enthusiasm. Nor does their zeal lessen as time passes and progress becomes barely perceptible. The mosque is a special endeavor, one that is dear to all Muslims because it is done for their Creator. Ordinary, financially strapped Muslims are consistently urged to give small amounts; over a period of time every local Muslim feels that he or she has a stake in the completion of "our" mosque.

Mustafiz, Alomgir's young assistant, joined our conversation just as Alomgir questioned me about my motherland. "Your president is Clinton, is it not so?" he ventured. I replied with a question: "Who is your president?" Neither of the *maulavis* could recall his name. Their expertise lies in religious matters. To their way of thinking, it is enough that humans attend to their Creator. What really matters in life is religion alone. I kidded the *maulavis* about being citizens of the eighth most heavily populated nation on earth, and yet they do not even know their president's name. The older *maulavi* excused this ignorance with a smile and a shrug. "It doesn't matter. Bangladesh is of no consequence in worldly affairs." Goaded by my teasing, however, the younger man searched his memory and soon came up with the correct answer. "Abdul Rahman Bishas is president," he stated seriously. This younger man does not share the attitude of the older one that such matters "make no difference."

In a recent mission publication, a Latin America-based missioner criticizes missionaries who work among Muslims but do not also try to convert them to Christianity. The American missioner does not think anyone does mission properly unless and until he orally announces the Gospel. Another missioner, this one working in Bangladesh, believes that we would be tossed out of the country if we tried that approach, that is, the direct oral proclamation of the Good News. I disagree with the criticism of the Latin missioner, while the comment of my fellow Bangladesh missioner seems irrelevant. For, even if the government and important Islamic leaders were urging missioners to preach their faith by word of mouth, and to campaign openly for adherents, I would continue to do as I have been doing precisely because I believe that it is the best way to communicate to Muslims what Christianity is. I am convinced that practical love for the poor and visible respect for all that they hold precious (that is, their religions, Islam or Hinduism) is the finest manner of conveying Christ's message. Service offered to the poor without expectation of getting anything in return for it (e.g., conversions) stuns the Muslim middle class and confounds their religious leadership. They say, and believe, "There is no disinterested person in this life." It is in seeing (and not merely hearing about) disinterested love for the poor that a wave of understanding washes over Muslims. Loving service to the forgotten sick and disabled poor is the most enlightening activity that I have been able to imagine during the past years in Bangladesh.

Moreover, I think that mission in Bangladesh is essentially signmaking. For this is a culture drenched in oratory. The people are inundated by eloquence. What is required now is for them to see the lived truth. As Jesus came to seek and to save the lost, so do I follow his method among the sick-poor. As my faith teaches, so I believe: Muslims are not lost; they have the same chance as do Christians to be saved by their goodness of life and concern for others. I seek out the physically lost, that is, those on the path to bodily death—to save them, to help them have a better life, and—not coincidentally—to illustrate for them Jesus' unselfish way.

Headmaster Matiur Rahman is the respected gentleman who originally invited me to come and live in Kishorganj. "We welcome a brother who will live among us in poverty and celibacy" he encouraged me. Now he is ailing, and stays in his house recovering from a hernia operation that took place some months back. When I visited him today he surprised me, saying, "I missed my chance to do as you are doing. Oh, of course, I have been spending myself usefully to run this high school for the past thirty-five years. And I helped found the Kishorganj Public Library. But all that is not as you are doing. I wish I could have worked along with you for those who have no hope of getting health care. But now, my health is broken." The headmaster is admired and respected throughout the town as a social worker, a term which carries connotations of generosity and self-sacrifice in Bangladesh.

The barber had just completed my haircut, but then it began to rain, so, instead of leaving the shop I sat on a stool in the doorway. An old newspaper held my attention. Soon, an argument between the man in the barber's chair and a man standing on the street broke out and I had to concentrate in order not to be distracted. After five minutes of not paying attention to them I realized that they were arguing about me. The barechested man in the chair was recounting the things he had seen me do for people. In response, the *maulavi* on the road was giving him a verbal lashing. The *maulavi*'s trump card was "*Namaz* [the formal prayer of Muslims] is *the* key to heaven!" That is to say, the exclusive key. The *maulavi* was announcing that, because Christians do not pray *namaz*, I had failed to do the one exercise necessary for entrance into paradise. When I finally looked up from reading, I saw how disgusted he was with me. Too bad. Some—by no means all—religious leaders are particularly prone to jealousy because the people (the ignorant masses, according to such *maulavis*) see that a non-Muslim is doing something for their welfare. Thus, the people speak favorably of him. It makes the *maulavi* feel slighted. He is certain that he knows the way to Allah, that is, through *namaz*, a quite particular form of worship. Anything else, such as works of mercy or moral uprightness, is, far and away, secondary.

For years I was not content when Christian friends spoke of my missionary work as an apostolate of dialogue. "I did not come to Bangladesh to do dialogue work," I hastened to remind them. "I came to serve the poor, to witness to Christ's love for the neediest, and to help my Muslim and Hindu neighbors in whatever way the Spirit leads me." My disinclination to have this effort described as dialogue stemmed from a connotation of the word. Dialogue suggests talking. And, since my involvement with Muslims and Hindus emphasizes action with and for the seriously ill among them, I did not wish to be labeled a talker—all the more so because, in Bangladesh, there is so much of permanent value that can be accomplished without much talking taking place. The teachings of Jesus that bring joy and peace to Christian hearts can be grasped by Muslims and Hindus only if they see us doing the works that Jesus did, that is, the works for which Muslims and Hindus also love Jesus. Thus, I preferred the words *servant*, *witness*, and *brother* to describe this mission.

If I chose to give priority to serving, rather than to speaking, it was not because of my modest language skills. Something else prodded me to be a doer of good deeds instead of a spokesperson for good ideas or a catalyst for good works by other persons. It was the conviction that my Muslim and Hindu neighbors read actions more clearly than texts, that they are moved by sympathy more deeply than by sermons, and that they respond more heartily to love than to stories about virtue.

Nowadays, I've noticed, there is more exactness than before when church people speak of dialogue. More and more, attention is directed toward "the dialogue of life." Deeper appreciation for dialogical living is being fostered in the Church. There is greater recognition of the dialogue that takes place when we live with one another, as when, for example, Christians live among Muslims and Hindus in Bangladesh. The dialogue goes on when we communicate our hopes and fears to one another, or when we speak about whatever is on our minds. The dialogue also goes on when we only observe others. Their every public action, their example—good and bad—reveals their character and their faith. Our actions and example reveal the same to them. Like it or not, we are partners with Muslims and Hindus in dialogue. In Bangladesh, a Christian can avoid dialogue only by absenting himself or herself from this environment wherein Muslims, Hindus, and Christians live side by side.

Thus, I live in a hut in an all-Muslim neighborhood in a small town, banter with men while bathing at the *ghat* [bathing place] or relaxing in tea stalls, pump tubewell water for children, haggle with store owners in the bazaar, cook on a one-burner kerosene stove while amused women watch and question, ride a bicycle along rural paths in search of the seriously ill, offer hope to the ailing and encouragement to their families, and provide daily explanations to numerous intensely curious inquirers who ask "Who are you? What do you do? Why do you do it?"

I tell them, "I am your Christian brother. I go about doing good and healing because that is what Jesus did. Jesus is my model; I am his follower."

If this is dialogue, I admit to doing it. Yet I prefer to call it mission.

For those who long to see improved relationships among the religions of the world, a statement from St. John is especially encouraging: God is greater than our hearts (1 John 3:20).

Similar to that statement are two others. Eye has not seen nor ear heard, nor has it entered into the heart of a human, what things God has prepared for those who love God (1 Corinthians 2:9). Nothing shall be impossible with God (Luke 1:37).

All three texts caution us: When thinking about God, do not be cautious. For God is inconceivably other than what we imagine. God is too good to be grasped by the mind. We cannot exaggerate God's mercy.

Our hearts crave love and peace. We need to recall that God is the author of that longing. We suppose that we reflect the large-mindedness of God whenever we tolerate persons belonging to other religions. But the Creator of all tolerance must smile at the stinginess of our generosity. God sustains all that is good in the world, including the jumble of religions. Grace should encourage us to scrutinize the hearts and lives of others and not to get bogged down in the teachings of the religions they profess. How little sense we have. How slow of heart we are to believe in the good will of others. All good things are possible for faithful Muslims, Hindus, Christians, and others who love the Almighty.

A Christian's mind may instruct his or her heart that the unity of peoples will be complete if and when they all believe in Jesus. But the heart knows that unity is possible now. Even at the moment when we profess vastly different beliefs, our hearts strain for unity and peace. God creates and sustains the straining. God also fulfills our longing, today.

Look at the goodness in others' lives. The man who acts in holiness is holy indeed (1 John 3:7). No one whose actions are unholy belongs to God (1 John 3:10), regardless of whether he is Christian, or Muslim, or whatever. In fact, whoever does what is good belongs to God (3 John 11).

If we really understand love—love as taught to us by God in Jesus—will we not lay down our very lives for others? Is not this giving of self to others for God's sake the purpose of Christian living? Is self-donation not also sufficient reason for missioners to live among non-Christians? When missioners go simply to live among and give themselves to others, it is enough. "The way we came to understand love was that he laid down his life for us; we, too, must lay down our lives for our brothers" (1 John 3:16). An adequate and excellent reason for mission work among non-Christians is the Spirit-inspired urge to lay down our lives for persons who need us.

Some missioners think that they have failed if they have won no converts to our Christian faith. They want to see conversion statistics. They feel a need—whether self-imposed or laid upon them by their sponsors—to fulfill a quota. They do not pursue God but, rather, an artificial objective. "Be on your guard against idols" (1 John 5:21) is a timely reminder.

As long as we love the people among whom God has placed us we should never fear that we are not doing enough for them or for the mission of the Church. In love there is no room for fear (1 John 4:18) or for the anxiety that we love too little. Love is the fulfillment of the law. It is also ample reason for being and continuing in mission.

I am sometimes asked about the relation between my contact with common people and the need for interreligious dialogue among scholars.

An educated Muslim friend tells me: "We Bengali Muslims believe all Englishmen abuse liquor and women and that they despise the poor. Our dramas illustrate that theme repeatedly. But what you are doing is amazing to us. We see that you do not drink. Women can safely come to you in time of illness and you will help them without demanding a reward. You actually love the poor."

Dialogue on this level, that is, on the Muslim neighborhood level, is important because of the perception Muslims have of Christian missionaries. They think missionaries have no other purpose than the conversion of Muslims. Educated Muslims often imagine that we missionaries approach the poor because they are vulnerable and can be bought. Another educated Muslim warned me at the outset of my dwelling among the poor in the town of Kishorganj: "Remember, we are watching you." Only recently did colonial history come to an end in Bangladesh. One legacy of the English colonial master is a deep suspicion among Muslims that the white man intends them no good.

There is no better way to convert the mind of an educated Muslim to benign thoughts toward Christianity than for the missioner to live among the poor and uneducated as a brother and a neighbor. If we wish to alter the misconceptions that the educated and relatively wealthy Muslims have of missionaries, the best we can do is to be with and for the poor. Middle-class, educated Muslims, i.e., those who influence society by their outlook and the expression of their views, observe our behavior and activities as closely as do the poor among whom we live. By spending ourselves among the poor we simultaneously affect the non-poor. Lifestyle and service say more to educated Muslims than any other sort of dialogue. If they do not see Christian foreign missioners humbly living among the Muslim poor, and serving them, then, I am convinced, no amount of vocal dialogue on the scholarly level will suffice to uproot the suspicion in their hearts. Both levels of dialogue are necessary, of course. But without lives of missionary witness which clearly illustrate Christian respect and love for the Muslim poor, then explanations, discussions, and eloquence will fail to penetrate hearts.

My hut is in a poor neighborhood surrounded by economically insecure day laborers and rickshaw pullers. The service I offer is reserved exclusively for the poor who are seriously ill. But I do have contact with the educated class. They see me on the streets and ask me "Who are you?" and "What are you doing here?" They come across me in the bazaar and inquire about my work and my diet. They see me at the local government hospital and ask me if I have a salaried job that obligates me to serve the sick. They encounter me at the tea stall, the bicycle parts store, the medicine shop, and the post office. They are curious and direct in questioning me. I try to answer every question. In a rudimentary way, every one of them becomes a dialogue partner.

After they have observed that I live with the poor and reserve my service exclusively for them, some of the educated ones chide me. "You are a *shabeb*, a white man. You come from an advanced country. Yet you live so simply. No electricity or cook. No automobile or servant to carry water. You are a big [important] person, so why do you submit to hardship?" Happily for me I do not always have to reply, because others have already gathered to listen to our conversation. "He is a dedicated person. The prophet Jesus lived this way, and he follows Jesus," someone in the crowd explains to the educated inquirer. What could be better than for the skeptical, educated Muslim to receive a totally correct answer from a person he thinks of as ignorant?

What is the importance of dialogue on this level? Simply put, it is that without Christian missioners who will live lives of service and uttermost simplicity among Muslims, no amount of dialogue between intellectuals will ever transform our relationship from that of suspicion to that of trust and friendship.

Leavetaking

It is three years since I came to this district town, and now is the time for me to consider my next move. Three years seems to be the ideal length of time for the purpose of Christian mission in Bangladesh. Friendship and trust have been born and allowed to grow. A more mature relationship now exists—the relationship of brother to brothers and sisters—and it is reinforced by periodic visits to my former homes. It has not been necessary to stay beyond three years in each place in order to accomplish this purpose. Moreover, if I did not move on to new towns, the benefits that derive from visiting old friends could not be gained.

Recently I visited the Tangail district—where I lived from 1977 until 1986. On a borrowed bicycle I spent six hours riding twenty miles through familiar villages. I enjoyed seeing old friends and they shared the sentiment. In the village of Sitki, Jamela was darker and thinner than I had ever seen her. She is worn out at age thirty, a widow and the mother of four daughters. Her oldest, Nur Jahan, is the most beautiful girl in the village, but already has been divorced for having failed to give her husband a bicycle as promised in their wedding contract. Jamela requested that someone go fetch Nur. When the stunning fifteen-year-old divorcee came running to meet me her mother was pleased that my attention remained mostly on herself.

In the village of Paikmuril, dozens of people chased after my bike until I stopped at a central place. Shefali's mother jested that I had forgotten the seven-year-old girl whose life I had once helped save. I had to admit to them all that I did not recognize amidst the crowd the daughter she spoke of. Laughingly her mother pulled a swath of cloth from the head of a child whom I had imagined to be a boy. Shefali's long, black hair fell down to her shoulders; she had been carrying dirt in a basket on her head and, until that moment, had looked like the little boys.

A quarter mile away from the Dhaleshwari River I stopped to take in the scene. A great, desolate, sandy expanse stretched before me. Hardly a person was in view; how rare a sight in over-packed Bangladesh. Sand hung in the air too, creating a haze over the starkly beautiful spot.

In the village of Bangun Tal I distributed photos to villagers so anxious to see themselves in the pictures that they risked ripping them. "Why did he return?" one uncomprehending person asked someone. "He misses us" was the answer volunteered by one who understands.

In the village of Hugra a crowd playfully seized my bicycle, forcing me to dismount. "Were you going to pass through without stopping to see us?" shouted the mother of a boy I had tried but failed to save. Her husband pleaded with me to rest awhile, but I was for going on. His attractive wife, in accordance with the custom of bosomy Bengali mothers, partially exposed her torso. She could have said: "Silver and gold I have none, but a fleeting glimpse of an exquisite breast I can give you." (I departed after taking due note of her display.)

In the village of Shantos I dropped in on the principal of the Boys' High School at the Islamic University. Mohammed Hossain was delighted to see me even though, by that time, I was a dirty visitor. "I always remember you, Bob Brother, and speak about your life of service," said he. Food was sent in by his wife. I begged to be excused because of the Ramzan fast. "But you are a Christian!" he laughed in protest. Then, leaning toward another visitor to his home, a Muslim gentleman, he asked gravely: "And what are we Muslims doing while the Christians show us such sympathy and respect? Where are we?"

Because my time is taken up with efforts for the sick and disabled who are virtually all poor and illiterate, there are few opportunities to relate to literate, economically secure Bangladeshis. During the annual celebration of Eid-ul-Fitr, therefore, I communicate with middle-class friends. This year's Eid message, enclosed in a colorful, locally made card, went out to 280 people. Written in Bangla, it reads:

"Among humankind the nearest in love to the Muslim Believers will thou find those who say 'We are Christians.'" (Fifth Surah of the Qur'an)

Dear Brothers and Sisters,

Eid greetings to Sunni Muslim friends from a Catholic Christian missionary, your Brother Bob. I pray for you and your loved ones that you have grown in your dedication to Allah during Ramzan. I ask the Merciful One to fill your hearts with benevolent thoughts toward all other people, and with peace.

Soon after this Eid celebration I shall leave Kishorganj. These past three years among you have been happy and satisfying years for me. I came to this district to do several things:

—to live with and for Bangladeshis, who I believe are my brothers and sisters, even though they are Muslims and Hindus while I am a Christian;

—to serve the sick-poor;

—to demonstrate the deep respect that Catholic Christianity has for Islam and Hinduism; and

—to explain to all who inquire the reason why I live as a brother to persons whose religion and nationality I do not share.

I live among you as a brother simply because the Compassionate

One inspires me to do so. I live this way because Jesus, the Model for a Christian life

—went about doing good and healing the sick

—came to humankind to serve and not to be served

—left us an example of accepting inconvenience, and even suffering, so that others might enjoy life more.

In brief, because Allah loves us all, I also strive to love everyone.

I thank the Best Giver that it has been possible in Kishorganj to show this love in a practical way. Many of you have encouraged me by your words and kindness. Some of you have actually cooperated with me in serving the sick-poor. I ask the Holy One to bless you richly for the goodness you have shown to me and to others. I shall continue to remember you with gladness and to pray for you.

Your brother,
Brother Bob

On the morning of my final day in Kishorganj, I informed my closest neighbors of my imminent departure. The day was also the annual Eid festival, and I was glad that people would be busy in their homes. Word of my going spread quickly. Perhaps the nicest parting tribute was paid by Bayejid, the young teacher at the Islamic *madrasha* [seminary] in our neighborhood. He appeared at the door as I was packing, shook my hand, and without a word squatted in the bare room to watch my leavetaking preparations with misty eyes.

Five persons had insisted on my eating with them today: Fatima and Shah Aziz, the district president of the Communist Party; Nurun Nahar, the director of the Girls' Orphanage; Shofiqul "Liton" who once told me "I love America"; Toyob Uddin of the Special Branch Police who has power to grant or to deny my yearly visa request; and the Deowan family—descendants of the original owners of all the land in Haybatnagar where I had lived during these past three years. Among that family are several educated, progressive, sports-minded young men. They brought to me the only Eid card I received this year, addressed: "We are for Bob Brother," as if I were a football club.

Just before shutting the door of my hut for the last time, I handed the lock and key to Shiraj, the owner. I was about to tell him how much I had enjoyed living in his little bamboo house, but he beat me to the draw.

"People in the town are talking," he said. "They say you've done a lot for the poor."

"All praise be to Allah," I responded.

Outside, Ayesha spoke for a small crowd of persons who had gathered to accept whatever house furnishings I wished to give away. She had come a bit too late to receive even an old calendar or an empty jar. When she spoke, however, she appeared to be satisfied: "No one has any demands to make on you," she said. Meaning: We will not hold you. You owe nothing to any of us. You are free to go.